HEIRS *and* LEGATEES
of
CAROLINE COUNTY
MARYLAND

Genealogical Extracts from the
Land Commission Records (1774–1895)
and County Chancery Court Records (1815–1863)

Irma Harper

HERITAGE BOOKS
2010

HERITAGE BOOKS

AN IMPRINT OF HERITAGE BOOKS, INC.

Books, CDs, and more—Worldwide

For our listing of thousands of titles see our website
at
www.HeritageBooks.com

Published 2010 by
HERITAGE BOOKS, INC.
Publishing Division
100 Railroad Ave. #104
Westminster, Maryland 21157

Other Heritage Books by Irma Harper:

Heirs and Legatees of Caroline County, Maryland
Kent County, Delaware Land Records, Volume 9: 1768–1772
Kent County, Delaware Land Records, Volume 10: 1772–1775

Other Heritage Books by F. Edward Wright and Irma Harper:

Maryland Eastern Shore Newspaper Abstracts, Volume 5: Northern Counties, 1825–1829
Maryland Eastern Shore Newspaper Abstracts, Volume 7: Northern Counties, 1830–1834

International Standard Book Numbers
Paperbound: 978-1-58549-126-1
Clothbound: 978-0-7884-8494-0

INTRODUCTION

This is a compilation of information taken from two excellent sources of genealogy: Land Commission records and Chancery Court documents. The Land Commission records are contained in bound volumes held by the courthouse. This book covers the entire period in which land commissions existed for Caroline County, beginning in 1774. The county chancery court records begin in 1815. At the present time both sets of records are held at the courthouse in Denton. Land commissions were established in response to petitions by persons seeking to officially establish the boundaries of their property or division of estates in the case of heirs inheriting an undivided parcel of real property. Such requests arose at the prompting of a dispute with owners of neighboring property, a desire to forestall future controversy or a need by surviving heirs to divide their inherited land.

The disappearance of a some landmark might well have justified the need to affirm the lines of the tract while there were still persons alive who remembered certain facts regarding the boundary. These deponents sometimes recalled events of the past of special interest to those following the history of one of the local families; they often mentioned members of families involved and their genealogy; and they stated facts about themselves, including their ages. Each commission record is identified by the month in which the court appointed the commission and the record book (A through F) followed by page number.

Likewise the chancery court records reveal information about the familes: the names and dates of death of individuals, names of children, ages of infants (persons under the age of 21) and names of their guardians - and other genealogy. Beginning on page 44 we present the record of the county chancery court docket with additional information taken from the actual chancery court record. The docket includes cases which were never heard in court and "struck off." The date of the docket is given at the end of each case entry. The dockets, the recorded cases and the actual papers from which the records were compiled are held at the courthouse.

Abbreviations used:

CAR - Caroline (County)
co - county
Com - Commission
dec'd - deceased
DOR - Dorchester (County)

ment: - mentioned
poss - possession
TA - Talbot (County)
Q.A. - Queen Anne's (County)

F. Edward Wright
Westminster, Maryland 1989

CAROLINE COUNTY, MARYLAND
LAND COMMISSION RECORDS

1774 August Court
A1 - William Polk, appointed by DOR court guardian to Mary Nutter, or-
phan of William Nutter, possessed with OTTOWOTTOCOQUIN in CAR.
Com: William Bradley, Jr; Robert Clarkson; James Richards; Thomas
White.
Ment: John Jessop; Charles Nutter; William Nutter the elder; David
Nutter.
James Ross, 71 years(1774) ment: Charles Nutter; William Nutter;
William Nutter the second, dec'd.
Robert Ross, 42 years(1774) ment: William Willson, dec'd.
David Williams, Sussex Co, DEL, 51 years(1775) ment: William Nutter;
John Nutter; William Owens.
William Ross, 31 years(1774) ment: William Nutter second.

1776 March Court
A7 - Henry Harrington re: JOSEPH'S LOTT depends on OLD TOWN.
Com: Richard Mason; Thomas Billingsley Keene; Thomas Hughlett;
Benson Stainton.
Richard Swift(Quaker) 69 years(1776) ment: his father, William
Swift; his brother, William Swift.
Thomas Baggs, 67 years(1776) ment: Henry Casson, Nathaniel Knotts;
his father, John Baggs; William Sheetle; Nicholas Goldsborough.
Phillip Harrington, 58 years(1776) ment: his father, Richard Harr-
ington.

1776 August Court
A10- John Tillotson and Henry Downes, Jr. re: PITTS VINEYARD
Com: Jeremiah Colston; Giles Hicks; Philip Feddeman, William
Dickinson.
John Cooper, 27 years(1775) ment: John Morgan
Giles Hicks, 56 years(1775) ment: old John Emory of Q.A. Co.

1776 November Court
A14- John Ashcum Hooper re: SHIELDS
Com: Joshua Clark, Jeremiah Colston, Giles Hicks, Abraham Collins.
Joseph Bland Sr., 57 years(1775) ment: Doctor Potter's landing;
Richard Webster, Thomas Causey, Capt. Andrew Price.
Jonathan Ireland, 51 years(1775) ment: Henry Ennalls surveyor of
DOR; William Ellis.
Mary Tull, 43 years(1775) ment: Edmond Melvel; Joseph Blackwell.
Solomon Causey, 40 years (1775) ment: Thomas Causey, dec'd; Richard
Webster; Capt. Andrew Price.
Ann Beacham, 40 years(1775) ment: Sarah Morgan; old John LeCompte;
John Pruett; John Hooper; Edward Rumbly.

1777 August Court
A17- William Winchester Mason re: DUDLEY'S CHANCE depends on CLYMERS
CHANCE and MULBERRY GARDEN.
Com: Joshua Clark; Nathaniel Potter; Jeremiah Colston; Henry
Downes Jr.
Ment: William Banning; James Climer; William Dickinson.
Giles Hicks, 57 years(1776)
Benjamin Cooper, 35 years (1776)
Thomas Hardcastle, 40 years (1776)

John Russom, 50 years (1776)
James Hicks, 62 years (1776)

1778 November Court
A23- Charles Nicols re: JONES FOREST
Com: Henry Downes, Jr; Giles Hicks; Jeremiah Colston; William
Hopper.
John Anthony of TA, 61 years(1778) ment: John Webb; John Webb's
son, John.

1779 March Court
A26- Jeremiah Colston re: LAMBERT
Com: Charles Daffin; William Dickinson; David Robinson; Richard
Loockerman.
John Russom, 50 years(1779) ment: his father ____; KIRKHAM'S
LOTT and KIRKHAM'S GARDEN.
Benjamin Cooper, 40 years(1779) ment: John Russom, the father of
John Russom.

1779 June Court
A29- Thomas Baggs re: CHANCEHITTS
Com: Thomas Hardcastle; Thomas Hughlett; Samuel Jackson; Peter
Harrington.
Laurance Everitt, 59 years(1779) ment: John Emory surveyor of Q.A.Co
Edward Slaughter, 52 years(1779) ment: old Laurance Everitt.

1780 March Court
A31- John Slaughter re: IRISH DISCOVERY
Com: Richard Mason; Thomas Goldsborough; Benjamin Sylvester;
Robert Hardcastle.
Jeremiah Monticue, 46 or 47 years(1779) ment: his father, William
Monticue; BAKER'S PLAINS.
Edward Everett of Q.A.Co, 65 years(1779) ment: James Countiss; John
Lane.
Thomas Baggs, 71 years(1779) ment: his father, _____.

1780 June Court
A34- William Bell re: PURNELL'S FOREST
Com: Henry Downes; Giles Hicks; David Robinson; Robert Casson.
John Purnell, 40 years(1779) ment: Thomas Jump of William; "the
old Boone's".

1781 March Court
A37- Thomas Noel re: THE RANGE and FRAZIER'S LOTT
Com: Nathaniel Potter; Henry Dickinson; Philip Walker; Joshua Willis
Ment: Ladmore's children; ____Sharpe; Tibbles Baggs; William Parker;
Croneen; James Murray's mill.
Peter Sharp Edmondson, 78 years(1780) ment: his bro, William Edmond-
son, dec'd; John Sharp, dec'd; Robert Sharpe.
John Richardson, 75 years(1780) ment: Charles Frazier, Andrew Russell
and CRONEEN'S LAND.
Isaac Cederson, 59 years(1780) ment: Moses Micols; Benjamin Edgell,
late of DOR; William Parker.
James Cederson, 61 years(1780) ment: Peter Carter; Samuel Colebourn.

1780 March Court
A42- Thomas Noel re: THE RANGE and FRAZIER'S LOTT

2

Com: Nathaniel Potter; Henry Dickinson; Philip Walker; Joshua Willis.
Ment: William Parker; William Ennalls.
John Stevens, 40 years(1780) ment: Alexander Frazier's land SARAH'S
DELIGHT and FRAZIER'S LOTT; William Haskins, surveyor.
Peter Sharpe Edmondson, 78 years(1780).
William Edmondson, 56 years(1780).

1774 August Court
A45- John Dwiggins re: LYFORD seized for term of one year by will of
William Webb, which descends to James Webb, son of Edgar, said
William Webb son of James, a minor.
Com: Jeremiah Colston; Aaron Downes; William Dickinson: Nathaniel
Potter.
Vinson Price, 56 years(1774) ment: SEWEL'S RANGE; William Eagle,
dec'd. of Q.A. Co.; Mager Sewel; old James Kirkham late QA dec'd;
James Kirkham.
Elizabeth Mills, 80 years(1774) ment: James Webb;s land; her husband,
David Mills.
Solomon Kenton(Quaker) 60 years(1775) ment: James Webb of Q.A.
Elizabeth Vinson, 51 years(1775) ment: her father, David Mills of
DOR.
Nathaniel Potter, 34 years(1775).

1781 June Court
A50- John Hooper re: SHIELDS
Com: Henry Dickinson; Giles Hicks; David Woolford; Maccabees Alford.
Nathaniel Potter, 39 years(1780) ment: Nevitt's land; John Young;
Thomas White, surveyor; William Haskin.
Joshua Wheeler, 53 years(1780) ment: Henry Webster; David Mills;
Capt. Andrew Price; Henry Davis.
Zabdiel Potter, 33 years(1780) ment: John Ashcomb Hooper; Thomas
and John Young; Robert Broidy.
Col. Vincent Price, 63 years(1780) ment: John Young of DOR, dec'd;
Henry Webster of DOR, dec'd.
Thomas White of Kent Co., DEL, 51 years(1780) ment: Edward Rumbly.

A53- Peter Webb of TA enters an Obligation & Award: John Hooper's bond
re: SHIELDS depends on TIVERTON.
William Edmondson and Joseph Foster arbitrators.

1780 October Court
A56- Henry Kemp re: WHEATLEY'S alias DANIEL'S FIELDS depends on TAYLOR'S
CHANCE.
Com: Charles Daffin; Robert Postlethwaite; Richard Loockerman; James
Seth.
Sharpless Cooper, 70 years(1781).

1782 June Court
A59- Thomas Bennett Willson, Esq., of Q.A. Co. re: SEWELL'S RANGE.
Com: Charles Daffin, William Dickinson; Philemon Downes; Richard
Loockerman.
Giles Hicks, 63 years(1782) ment: Thomas Wilson; old John Emory.
Deposition taken in presence of Col. Vincent Price; John Swiggins;
Aaron Downes; David Vincent; Col. William Hopper; Hawkins Downes.
John Dwiggans, 46 years(1782)
Wheatley Wadman, 56 years(1782) ment: William Banning

Solomon Eagle, 60 years(1782)
Col. Vincent Price, 63 years(1782)
Jeremiah Colston, 57 years(1782)
Thomas Leverton, 24 years(1782)

1782 March Court
A64- Nehemiah Cooper re: PARTNERSHIP
Com: Philemon Downes; Robert Postlethwaite; Robert Casson: David
Robinson.
William Roe, 50 years(1782) ment: Jonathan Bartlett; Jacob Boon;
Abel Chilton Sr.

1782 March Court
A66- Peter Edmondson son of Peter of KENT CO. re: RICHARDSON'S CHOICE
Com: Henry Dickinson; Philip Walker; Zabdiel Potter; William Frazier
Nehemiah Andrew, 53 years(1782) ment: heirs of John Nicols of DOR,
dec'd; Mary Fleetwood; Isaac Nicols uncle to John; Isaac Nicols'
grand dau, Elizabeth Andrew wife of Anderton Brown.
John Richardson Sr, 77 years(1782) ment: Thomas Perry of DOR, dec'd.
John Willis, Sr., 51 years(1782) ment: his mother, Elizabeth Willis,
dec'd; his father, John Willis, DOR, dec'd; "old Nicols".
William Edmondson, 57 years(1782) ment: John Nicols son of John
Nicols; Richard Collison; his uncle, Isaac Nicols; Lydia Nicols,
wid of John Nicols son of John.
Thomas Conner, 50 years(1782) ment: Henry Nicols son of John, dec'd;
Andrew McGhee of DOR; William Stevens; Charles Dickinson; William
Haskins; William Edmondson; Peter Edmondson, Sr.; Robert Hardikin;
Joshua Willis, Sr.

1782 October Court
A73- William Bell re: PURNALL'S ADDITION depends on PURNALL'S FOREST
Com: Charles Daffin, Henry Downes, David Robinson, Robert Casson.
Stone was set in presence of William Bell; William Purnall; John
Roe; Asa Banning; Thomas Purnall; William Purnall Jr.; John Thawley;
Richard Purnall; Edward Thawley; Robert Nevill; Purnall Jump; James
Purnall; Sylvester Purnall; Andrew Purnall; William Anthony; Alemby
Jump; William Jump.
Benjamin Whitbey, 52 years(1782) ment: his father, William Whitbey;
Margaret Banning.
John Purnall, 43 years(1782).
John Williams, 38 years(1782) ment: Anthony Roe; CASTLETOWN; Matthew
Chilton.
John Thawley, 28 years(1782).
Edward Thawley, 38 years(1782) ment: his father, John Thawley.
Peter Jump, 53 years (1782) ment: his father, Thomas Jump.

1782 June Court
A78- Peter Jump re: COLNE RECTIFIED
Com: Charles Daffin; Henry Downes; David Robinson; Robert Casson.
Stone was set in presence of Philemon Downes; William Shepherd;
Elijah Jump; John Barwick; Solomon Jump; Thomas Russom; John Will-
iams; Henry Snow; William Keets; Peter Jump; James Mason.
Ment: Absalom Knotts; James and Philip Ward.
Benjamin Jump, 40 years(1782) ment: Jacob Wooters; Thomas Jump;
Littleton Ward; Henry Pollock.
William Shepherd, 39 years(1782) ment: Thomas Alkin.
Elijah Jump, 32 years(1782) ment: LAYNES ADDTN; James Layne.

4

1782 March Court
A84- Elizabeth Stainton and Margaret Campbell re: DENTON'S VALLEY
Com: Matthew Driver, Thomas Hughlett, Samuel Jackson, Henry Downes
William Skinner, DEL, 52 years(1782) ment: "old Richard Smith;
old John Lane; Old Peter Rich some 30 years ago; old Nathaniel
Smith.
Judal Draper, 58 years(1782).
Thomas White, KENT CO., DEL., 52 years(1782) ment: John Campbell,
dec'd.
Robert Dixon, DEL., 37 years(1782) ment: Patrick Bwin(?).

A88- Vincent Price re: ANDREW & PRUDENCE'S SATISFACTION alias TODCASTER
depends on STEVENS FIELDS.
Com: Zabdiel Potter, Henry Dickinson, Philip Walker, John Stevens.
Ment: William Robinson, dec'd.
George Bell, 45 years(1782) ment: Robert Jordan, dec'd.; William
Purnal; old Solomon Robinson.
John Smith of Watts Creek, CAR.(Quaker), 82 years(1782) ment: Col.
Coursey; Capt. Andrew Price; Mrs. Elizabeth Lowe.
Nicholas Price, 52 years (1782) ment: John Layne of QA; deponent's
mother; Doctor Bullen's wife; Walter Layne.
Giles Hicks, 63 years(1782) ment: heirs of Joshua Clark; Henry
Clift; John Emory of QA; CATTE'S PLANTATION; Arthur Emory surveyor
of QA.
Aaron Downes, 48 years(1782) ment: Thomas Barron surveyor of CAR.
John Dwiggans, 46 or 47 years(1782) ment: Timothy Price; Mrs. Clark.
David Robinson, 49 years(1782) ment: he was guardian to William
Robinson; Bazil Warfield surveyor of QA.
James Hicks, 67 years(1782).

1783 June Court
A98- Robert Casson re: JUMP'S CHANCE depends on POCATY RIDGE.
Com: Philemon Downes, Henry Downes, William Hopper, Thomas Penning-
ton.
Peter Jump, 54 years(1783) ment: his aunt, Susanna Jump; her son,
Thomas Jump; Vaughn Jump, my cousin; Thomas Swan.
Benjamin Jump, 40 years(1783) ment: Thomas Jump son of William;
James and Thomas Bell; my grandfather, Thomas Jump.
James Curtis, 36 years(1783).
William Jump, 38 years(1783).
Thomas Swan, 66 years(1783) ment: old Thomas Swan; George Porter;
Robert Norris Wright; John Emory.
Depositions taken in presence of: Robert Casson, James Roddis(?),
Nathan Falconer, John Carpenter, William Gordon, John Jump, David
Casson, Aaron Floyd, Thomas Wootters, James Casson, Nathan Downes.

1783 October Court
A104-Charles Daffin re: KILRAY and KILRAY'S ADDITION.
Com: William Hopper, Richard Loockerman, Jacob Loockerman, Neal Price.
Sharpless Cooper, 73 years(1782) ment: old Thomas Forkner; Thomas
Meeds.
James Curtis, 36 years(1783) ment: his father-in-law John Cooper;
THE BEGINNING; John Meeds.
Rebeccah Cooper, 70 years(1783) ment: her husband, old John Cooper.
Taken in presence of _____ Casson, Thomas Cooper, John Cooper,
Henry Nicols, William Gordon, Thomas W. Meeds, John Meeds, David
Morgan of Bennett.

1783 October Court
A107-William Robinson and Henry Clift re: STEVENS HIS FIELDS
    Com: Charles Daffin, Henry Downes, Robert Postlethwaite; Robert
    Casson.
    Joshua Clark of TA(Quaker), 43 years(1783) ment: his father; also
    John Fountain and _____ Lane.
    Robert Kirby of TA, 56 years(1783) ment: Mary Bane; Walter Lane.
    Aaron Downes, 48 years(1783) ment: LANE'S FOLLY.
    Col. Vincent Price, 64 years(1783) ment: John Emory, surveyor;
    Thomas Bright; William Pollock; Mrs. Clark; William Robinson.
    Taken in presence of: Richard Loockerman, David Robinson, Marcy
    Fountain of John, William Banning, Richard Mason, James Bell, John
    Fountain, Jr., Walter Lane, Timothy Price.
    John Hobbs, 52 years(1783) ment: John Lane; Edward Clark; Mary Bane;
    John Sylvester; William Banks; Nathaniel Knotts.
    David Vinson, _____(1783) ment: Mr. Warfield.
    Capt. Nicholas Price, 52 years(1783).
    Charles Manship, 76 years(1783) ment: John Bracco.
    John Dwiggans, 48 years(1783) ment: Robert Floyd
    Samuel Williams, 52 years(1783).
    Mary Hobbs, 43 years(1783) ment: her mother.
    Taken in presence of: Aaron Downes, Philemon Downes, Major Middleton,
    John Hobbs Jr., George Dudley, Henry Clift Jr., Thomas Bright, Will-
    iam Clift, Hugh Rice.

1782 October Court
A112-Christopher Driver re: LLOYDS REGULATION which includes three ancient
    tracts, RATTLESNAKE RIDGE, PETERS PARK and HOBBS KINDNESS.
    Com: Joseph Richardson, William Whiteley, Peter Rich, John Stevens of
    Jonathan.
    Ment: Thomas Smith; FLETCHERS LANDING, Jeremiah Rhodes.
    Joshua Hobbs, 54 years(1783) ment: Robert Hobbs; Mary Hobbs; Thomas
    Pearson, all dec'd; John Morgan, dec'd.
    John Morgan, 44 years(1783)ment: Charles Hynson, dec'd.
    John Smith(Quaker) 82 years,(1783) ment: Edward Mathers(?); JAMES
    PARK now PETERS PARK.
    James Powel, SUSSEX CO, DEL., 68 years(1783)ment: Robert Hobbs, Henry
    Ennals Sr. surveyor of DOR.

1782 March Court
A119-Philemon Downes and his wife, Elizabeth, and Henry Downes and his
    wife, Margaret (in right of their wives) re: BAYNARDS LARGE RANGE
    ADDITION, PITTS VINEYARD and JOANS THICKETT.
    Com: Charles Daffin, Neal Price, Robert Casson, Thomas Pennington.
    Henry Casson, 73 years(1782) ment: Esther Baynard relict of Thomas
    Baynard; Thomas Roe; Mrs. Anthony Roe; Mrs. Feddeman.
    Thomas Baynard, KENT CO DEL., 70 years(1782) was born in the house
    which stands and did stand about 150 years, lived there until he was
    20 years of age. (was son of Thomas Baynard).
    Elizabeth Feddeman, 73 years(1782) ment: Robert Jones.
    Robert All, 34 years(1782) ment: Jonathan Wooters; Daniel Cox.

1783
A   Philemon Downes in right of his wife and as guardian to John Tillot-
    son, orphan, and John Cooper and William Webb re: division line be-
    tween PITTS VINEYARD and WEBBS CHANCE. Stone planted in presence of:
    Nathan Downes, John Dwiggins, William Stewart, John Tillotson, Nathan

Dwiggins, James Cooper, Thomas Tillotson, Thomas Cooper of John,
Henry Cooper, John Cooper of Thomas and Hannah Thompson.

1782 October Court
A124-Peter Collison and William Collison re: ENNALLS ENTRANCE.
    Com: John Ashcomb Hooper, David Woolford, John Stevens of Jonathan,
    James White.
    Thomas Dukes, 46 years(1783) ment: _____Ennalls.
    Cornelius Johnson, 43 years(1783) ment: Evin Rees; Thomas Dukes Sr.

1782 October Court
A128-Michael Smith re: SMITHS DISCOVERY
    Com: Charles Daffin; Jeremiah Colson, Richard Loockerman, Robert
    Casson.
    Sharpless Cooper, 73 years(1783).
    Taken in presence of: James Dwiggans , Whittington Meeds, Joseph
    Foster, Nathan Dwiggans.

1784 March Court
A132-Zabdiel Potter re: LAZY HILL depends on SHIELDS
    Com: Henry Dickinson, William Richardson, John Stevens, Joshua Willis
    Jonathan Ireland, 59 years(1784) ment: John Hooper; Capt. Zabdiel
    Potter; Henry Ennalls Jr. surveyor of DOR; William Ellis(called Great
    Billy Ellis).
    Anne Beauchamp, widow, 59 years(1784) ment: her father, John Young;
    John Lecompte, dec'd; Capt. Andrew Price; and John Pruet, both dec'd;
    old Sarah Davis; Edmond Melvill; Edward Rumbly.
    Mary Tull, 58 or 59 years(1784) ment: Thomas Nevitt's land.
    Solomon Causey, 49 years(1784) ment: Thomas Causey, dec'd; Richard
    Webster, dec'd; Capt. Andrew Price.
    David Woolford, 38 years (1784) ment: ELLIS'S VENTURE; Daniel Edgell;
    Joseph Blackwell; Jonathan Ireland.
    Ment: Richard Lyden's house.

1783 October Court
A139-Levin Jump of KENT CO. re: KNOTTS RANGE
    Com: Henry Downes, Robert Casson, Neal Price, Thomas Pennington.
    Peter Jump, 54 years(1784) ment: his brother, Thomas Jump; old
    Nathaniel Knotts; John Emory, surveyor.

1784 June Court
A143-Thomas Smith son of Ralph re: APPERLY & SURVEYOR'S FOREST. William
    Summers, tenant.
    Com: Joseph Richardson, Zabdiel Potter, John Allen Sangston, John
    Stevens of Jonathan.
    Edward Smith, 62 years(1783) ment: George Graham; John Arnet;
    Fletcher's bounded tree.
    Joshua Hoobs(Hobbs?), 51 years(1783) ment: Jonathan Hoobs(Hobbs);
    Solomon Hoobs(Hobbs?); John Morgin.

1784 October Court
A148-Matthew Driver re: RANGE
    Com: Thomas Hughlett, William Whitely, Peter Rich, Massey Fountain.
    Thomas White, KENT CO DEL, 55 years(1784) ment: his father, John White;
    Joshua Dines; Matthew Driver, Sr., James Lecompte, Sr.
    John White, CAR, 57 years(1784) ment: his father, John White; Joshua
    Dines; John Casson; John White(now known as John White, Irish); Robert

7

Rawley; James Lecompte, Sr; Matthew Driver Sr.
Thomas Baynard, KENT CO DEL, 73 years(1784) ment: Henry Ennalls;
Matthew Driver; Charles Lecompte; James Lecompte.
William Pritchard, SOM CO, 66 years(1784) ment: John White; old
John Shehaun.
Samuel Giles, 64 years(1784) ment: John Casson; James Lecompte.

A155-William Richardson and Henry Dickinson enter following depositions
and certificate re: BURFORD'S CLOSE (or BAKERS LAND) owned by George
Plater Esq.
Above record found in Joshua Clark and Nathaniel Potter's papers
(commissioners) - case having been interrupted by late war.
Anne Allen, 66 years(1774) ment: husband, Thomas Allen of DOR CO;
James Morgan; Sarah Davis; widow Cooper.
Moses Cranor, 41 years(1774) ment: widow Cooper, John Morgan of DOR.
Solomon Hobbs, 53 years (1774) ment: father, Robert Hobbs, of DOR;
William Harper, late DOR.
Joseph Foster, a Nichclite(1774) no age given, ment: his father,
Thomas Foster of DOR.
Taken in presence of Joshua Clark, Nathaniel Potter, William Rich-
ardson, Peter Adams, George Stockly, John Stevens, William Cary,
John Dwigans, Henry Dickinson, Joshua Hobbs, James Smith, Thomas
Swiggott, Daniel Nutterwell.
John Smith Sr., 74 years(1775) ment: Samuel Fountain; Peter Rich of
DOR.
John Pert, ship carpenter, 45 years(1776) ment: Jonathan Hobbs of
DOR; his father, Robert Hobbs; RATTLESNAKE RIDGE; old James Hignutt;
Samuel Dickinson.

1785 March Court
A162-George Plater Esq. re: BURFORD'S CLOSE, BURFORD'S HOPE and PLATER'S
ADDITION.
Com: Zabdiel Potter, Henry Dickinson, Philip Walker, David Woolford.
Joseph Foster, 47 years(1784), ment: father, Thomas Foster of DOR;
Jonathan Hobbs, son of Robert Hobbs.
Thomas White, KENT CO DEL, 54 years(1784) ment: Edward Lloyd of TA;
SHADWELL; Jonathan Hobbs and his father, Robert Hobbs.
Joshua Hobbs, 51 or 51 years(1784) ment: his father, Robert Hobbs;
RATTLESNAKE RIDGE: Jonathan Hobbs, son of Robert; Ann Allen; Michael
Lucus; Richard Quinnerly.
John Smith Sr., 84 years(1784) ment: Samuel Fountain; Peter Rich of
DOR.

A168-Charles Daffin re: HACTON and REDFORD.
Com: Philemon Downes, Henry Downes, Richard Loockerman, Jacob Loock-
erman.
Benoni Watson of TA, 49 years(1784) ment: Bennett Morgan; William
Webb; James Coker, free negro; Thomas Evans.
Taken in presence of Charles Daffin, Charles Nicols, Henry Nicols,
Thomas Meeds, John Dwiggins, Thomas Cooper, son of William.
Henry Downes, 37 years(1784) ment: Bennett Morgan; JONE'S FOREST.
Taken in presence of Charles Daffin, Charles Nicols; Thomas Meeds;
William Burton; Henry Martindale.
James Dwiggins of QA, 43 years(1784) ment: Bennett Morgan; William
Nicols.
Taken in presence of Charles Daffin, Charles Nicols, William Burton
Nathan Dwiggins.

1785 June Court
A172-Levin Caulk re: FAIR DEALING
  Com: John Stevens Marsh; John Ashcom Hooper; James White; David'
  Woolford.
  Thomas White, KENT CO DEL, 55 years(1785) ment: William Causey Sr.;
  Michael Todd; SEXTON'S LAND.
  Jesse Grayless, 47 years(1785) ment: Levin Caulk; Jesse Hubbart.
  Michael Todd, 52 years(1785).
  Betchim Causay, 45 years(1785) ment: Jesse Hubart.

1785 October Court
A177-James Hicks re: EDMONDSON'S GREEN CLOSE.
  Com: Richard and Jacob Loockerman, William Robinson, Jeremiah Col-
  ston.
  Michael Smith, 56 years(1785) ment: John Clement; James Hicks; his
  father, John Clement; old James Hicks.
  Taken in presence of John Russum, William Burton, Samuel Neal, Aaron
  Downes.
  Benjamin Cooper, 52 years(1785) ment: James Hicks; John Clement; John
  Russum.
  William Steward, 41 years(1785) ment: John Clement; John Russum; John
  Meeds; Vincent Clement; James Hicks.

1786 March Court
A181-Jacob Boon re: BOON'S PARK
  Com: Benedict Brice, Robert Postlethwaite, David Robinson, Benjamin
  Sylvester.
  Richard Fisher, 50 years(1784) ment: Jacob Boon, son of James.
  William Boon Sr., 51 years(1784) ment: William Bankes; John Maynor;
  WHITBY'S HAZZARD; Jacob Boon, James Tolson, William Rich; HICKORY
  RIDGE.
  Absalom Chance, 42 years(1784) ment: James Tolson; John Riddu; John
  Brown; Stephen Kirby; Jacob Boon.
  Joseph Rouse Sr., 64 years(1784) makes several depositions, ment:
  Jacob Boon; William Starky; Isaac Boon.
  Moses Boon, 42 years(1784) gave several depositions, ment: his
  father, Isaac Boon; Jacob Boon; John Lane Sr.; George Ford; Thomas
  Roe; James Andrew; Joseph Andrew; Joseph Boon; Hawkins Boon; James
  Boon; old Thomas Jump.
  James Boon Sr., 37 years(1784) ment: his father, Isaac Boon; Joseph
  Rouse; his uncle, Jacob.
  William Boon Jr., 48 years(1784) gave several depositions, ment: his
  father, Isaac Boon; old John Lane; Thomas Roe; Joseph Whitby.
  Persons present were: William Love, Joseph Boon, Joseph Whitby,
  Isaac Boon, William Clark, Moses Boon of Moses, Thomas Faulkner,
  Anthony Cox Jr., Benjamin Whitby Jr.
  John Whitby, KENT CO DEL, 59 years(1784) ment: Abraham Boon, a bro
  to old Jacob Boon; Moses Boon; William Boon; one Griffith; Nathan
  Jump, son of Thomas.
  Capt. Samuel Jackson, 59 years(1784) ment: Isaac Boon, bro of Jacob
  Boon.
  Benjamin Whitby, 52 years(1784) ment: William Banckes; Nathaniel
  Knotts.
  Peter Jump, 55 years(1786) ment: Joseph Rouse Sr., Arthur Emory and
  his father, John Emory; James Tolson; William Starky; James Boon Sr;
  Jacob Boon Sr.; Thomas Bell; Benjamin Townsend.

William Boon Jr., 49 years(1786) ment: his father, Isaac Boon; Peter
Jump. Present was Peter Jackson of Samuel.

A189-David Fountain re: EDMONDSON'S RESERVE
Com: David Woolford, John Ashcom Hooper, Philip Walker, Andrew
Satterfield.
Jonathan Ireland, 61 years(1785) ment: Peter Taylor Sr.; George
Hughes; William Harvey; COCIAIS FIELD.

A192-Charles Goldsborough Jr. of DOR re: THE WILDERNESS, SKIPTON, WAKEFIE
THE GORE, BENJAMIN'S DESIRE, FOX HILL, BETSYS CARE, ADDITION TO THE
PLAINS PART, RICHARDSON CHOICE, PERRYS PURCHASE PART and CANAAN.
Com: Henry Dickinson, Philip Walker, William Richardson, William Fra
ier.
John Willis, 53 years(1785) ment: SMITH'S POINT.
Ellis Thomas, 29 years(1785) gave several depositions, ment: his gra
father, John Richardson; John Winslow an orphan boy; Thomas Perry.
John Richardson, 45 years(1785) ment: his father(no name given); Joh
Harris, son of John Harris; William Ennalls; HUNTINGTON and WAKEFIEL
Peter Edmondson, 83 years(1785) ment: Samuel Dickinson, Edward Alfor
William Perry of Richard, 48 years(1785) gave several depositions,
ment: his brother, Thomas Perry; Edward Trippe; Charles Dickinson;
William Haskins; Alexander Frazier; Joseph Alford; John Harris; Jose
Bowdle; John Richardson.
John Mitchell, son of Ambrose, 35 years(1785) gave several depositio
ment: old John Richardson, Harrises land; Thomas Alford; Wm. Ennalls
John Willis, 53 years or 54 years(1785) gave several depositions,
ment: John Richardson Sr.; Mary Holland; William Jones; Benjamin
Nicolls; LUCK IN A BAG; James Edmondson; Barrow, the surveyor; Andre
Russell.
John Richardson, Nicholite or New Quaker, 45 years(1785) ment: his
father, John Richardson; John Nicols; John Willis.
Robert Hardikin of DOR, 52 years(1785) ment: Joseph Bowdle; Thomas
Bowdle, son of Joseph; Thomas Alford; Benoni Frazier.
Henry Carey, TA, 67 years(1785) ment: Thomas Dill of DOR; Charles
Dickinson; Alexander Frazier.
William Edmondson, Quaker, 60 years(1786) ment: Isaac Nicols; Joseph
Alford.
Persons ment: Samuel McGee; Thomas Perry; Richard Collison.

1786 June Court
A209-John Slaughter re: IRISH DISCOVERY
Com: Thomas Hardcastle, Thomas Goldsborough, Benjamin Sylvester,
David Robinson.
Thomas Bennett, KENT CO DEL, 55 years(1782) ment: BAKER'S PLAINS;
William Hughlett; Nathan Harrington, Capt. Thomas Hughlett.
William Harrington, 49 years(1782) ment: Benson Stainton; James Genn;
Capt. Thomas Hughlett.
Josiah Genn, 32 years(1782) ment: James Genn; Capt. Thomas Hughlett.
Mary Genn, 42 years(1782) ment: her husband, James Genn; Capt. Hugh-
lett.
Joseph Rouse, 63 years(1782) ment: Capt. Hughlett; William Hughlett;
Nathan Harrington; Thomas Bennett.
Thomas Baggs, 73 years(1782).
Nathan Harrington, son of Nathan, 27 years(1782).
Rebeccah Cox, 60 years(1782) ment: her father, John Lane, son of John

10

Anthony Cox, 64 years(1782) ment: John Lane son of John.
Arthur Emory of Q.A., 50 years and upwards(1782) ment: his father
(un-named); old Jacob Boon.
Bachelor Chance, Quaker, 61 years(1782).
Elizabeth Chance, Quaker, 62 years(1782) ment: Betty Carol's branch;
Genn's branch; James Genn.
Sarah Morgan, 50 years(1782) ment: her father, James Countiss.
Arnold Blades, 28 years(1782) ment: his father, James Blades; old
John Lane, Sarah Monticue.
Daniel Hughs, 36 years(1782) ment: James Blades; James Genn.
Samuel Jackson, 56 years(1782) ment: William Monticue; Edward Rich-
ards; BLOOMSBERRY.
William Eubancks, 46 years(1782) ment: James Countiss; DUBLIN.
Edward Everitt of Q.A., 66 years(1782) ment: William Monticue;
GOLDEN GROVE.
Francis Price of KENT CO DEL., 63 years(1782) ment: Robert Dixon;
James Countiss; old Obediah Dixon.
John Potts, taylor, 36 years(1782) ment: William Moore; old James
Blades.
Meremiah Monticue, 45 years(1782) ment: his father(un-named); his
"cozen" William Monticue; Edward Richards; Archibald Jackson;
Edward Garrett; James Blades.

1786 October Court
A219-Frederic Causey re: HOG ISLAND
   Com: Joshua Willis, Stephen Fleharty, Peter Edmondson, Philip
   Walker.
   Joseph Mullikin, 35 years(1785) ment: John Richardson; CARTERS land.
   George Murphey of DOR, 27 years(1786) ment: his father, James Mur-
   phey(tenant of Capt. Thomas Noel); BENNETTS PURCHASE; James Waters
   (tenant on HOGG ISLAND); Peter Steel; Foster Goldsborough.
   Peter Steel, 59 years(1786) ment: Jeremiah Carter; Foster Goldsbor-
   ough; Joseph Mullikin; William Frazier; William Perry.
   John Carter, 51 years(1786) ment: Alexander Frazier; Thomas White;
   Nicholas Goldsborough.

A226-John Fisher of Q.A. re: LAMBERT'S ADDITION and LAMBERT
   Com: Philemon and Henry Downes, Neal Price, Solomon Kenton of
   Solomon.
   John Russum, 56 years(1786) gave several depositions, ment: his
   father, John Russum; William Banning; Jeremiah Colston; Giles Hicks;
   old John Lane. Taken in presence of John Fisher, Jeremiah Colston,
   Solomon Eagle, William Colston, John Cooper Jr.
   Solomon Eagle, 64 years(1786) ment: his father(un-named); WOOLVERTON;
   Jeremiah Colston; Giles Hicks; John Russum.
   Col. Vincent Price, 68 years(1786) ment: Jeremiah Colston; KIRKHAM'S
   LOTT; William Banning; Timothy Lane; William Eagle; Thomas Leverton.
   Thomas Leverton of TA, 28 years(1786) ment: old Giles Hicks.

A233-Elijah Vinson re: CHESTNUT RIDGE
   Com: Christopher Driver, John Allen Sangston, Massey Fountain,
   Michael Lucas.
   Thomas Swiggett, 57 years(1785) of DOR ment: Edward Ross; James
   Vinson's land.
   Henry Swiggett, 55 years(1785, Nicholite, gave several depositions,
   ment: Peter Ross, dec'd; Thomas Swiggett; John Stevens; Thomas
   Barrow.

11

Edward Smith, 63 years(1785), gave several depositions, ment: his father, William Smith; MT. PLEASANT; Edward Ross.
William Stevens, Nicholite, 52 years(1785) ment: Edward Ross.
Allen Connerly, 47 years(1785).
Joseph Richardson, Jr., 40 years(1785) ment: Thomas Baynard's long field.
William Kelly, Nicholite, no age given(1785) ment: William Stevens.
Solomon Warren, 38 years(1785) ment: Allen Connerly.
Edward Willoughby, 42 years(1785).
Major Berry, 42 years(1785) ment: William Stevens and his bro, John Stevens; Thomas Baynard.

A244-William Stewart re: CAREY'S DISCOVERY
Com: Henry Downes, Solomon Kenton of Solomon, Henry Sharp, David Robinson.
Athel Stewart, 45 years(1786) ment: Solomon Kenton; GRAVELLY HOWE; his father, Thomas Stewart.
Nathan Wheatley, 48 years(1786) ment: Thomas Loveday; Thomas Kenton.
James Kenton, 47 years(1786), taken in presence of Neal Price, William Stewart, John King, Samuel Martindale, Nathan Wheatley, Jacob Pratt, Henry Stewart.
Jacob Pratt, 28 years(1786) ment: James Emory
Robert Hardcastle, 47 years(1786) ment: John Pickirin, son-in-law to James Kenton; Thomas Kenton son of said James.

A252-John Cooper re: WEBBS CHANCE and PITTS VINEYARD
Com: Robert Postlethwaite, Robert Casson, Neal Price, Solomon Kenton.
John Dwiggans, 49 years(1784) ment: his mother; Thomas Baynard.
Taken in presence of Durdin Orrell, David Morgan, Thomas Cooper of John, Henry Cooper of John.

A255-William Morgan and James Aaron re: END OF CONTROVERSY
Com: Zabdiel Potter, Peter Edmondson Jr., Joshua Willis, Stephen Fleharty. Ment: ALLCOCK'S MILL and JOHN STEVEN'S MILL.
Caleb Clark, 40 years(1786) ment: Joseph Blades, dec'd; Richard Webster, dec'd.
Thomas Blades, 33 years(1786).
John Cromeen, 39 years(1786).
William Sharp, 29 years(1786)
James Sharp, 26 years(1786)
David Woolford, 40 years(1786) ment: Peter Taylor
Levin Blades, 31 years(1786).
William Greenhawk, 66 years(1786) ment: Burtonwood Allcock.

A262-Charles Blair re: RETALLIATION depends on PINEY POINT.
Com: Peter Edmondson, Philip Walker, David Woolford, Joshua Willis.
Maccabees Alford, 53 years(1786) ment: William Haskins, survey of DOR; William Webster; my bro, Edward Alford.
Richard Clark, 43 years(1786) ment: Joseph Alford

1788 October Court
A268-Joshua Chilcutt re: PARTNERSHIP HAZZARD
Com: Charles Emory, Robert Postlewhait, Ezekiel Hunter.
William Bell, 52 years(1788) ment: Arthur Emory, John Roe, BROUGHTON.
William Stuart, 44 years(1788) ment: old John Cooper; Solomon Kenton; David Robinson; DRUM FIELD; Sacht(?) Jones; MARTINDALES HOPE; ANGLE.

12

1789 March Court
A274-John Fountain re: LAIN'S FOLLY depend on BENNETT'S TOLSON and STEP-
HEN'S FIELDS now in poss of Richard and Jacob Loockerman.
   Com: Philemon Downes, Henry Downes, Aaron Downes, William Robinson,
John Dickinson.
   John Hobbs, 58 years(1788) ment: Edward Clark; John Lane; John Syl-
vester; Mary Bayn; heirs of Walter Lane who owned LANE'S FOLLY.
   James Hicks, 73 years(1788) ment: Arthur Emory; John Loockerman.
   Mary Hobbs, 47 years(1788) ment: Mary Bayn and her bro, Walter Lane;
Henry Clift.
   Aaron Downes, 54 years(1788).
   James Hicks also ment: William Banckes; Nathaniel Knotts; Henry Downes
Francis Orrell, 67 years(1788).
   Ment: in commissioner's report were FOUNTAIN'S landing or grainery;
William Robinson's plantation, CATTS; Giles Hicks.

1789 June Court
A282- Charles Daffin re: DAFFIN FARM RESURVEYED
   Com: Henry Downes, John Hardcastle, Thomas Barrow, Neal Price, Solo-
mon Kenton.
   Burton Falkner, 67 years(1789) ment: William McNeice; Webb's land;
REDSTONE; John Webb.
   William Burton, 55 years(1789) ment: REDFORD(Webb's land); John Gib-
son; Howes Goldsborough; Samuel Thomas; Henry Martindale; Charles
Nicols' heirs.
   Benjamin McNeice, 32 years(1789) ment: his father, William McNeice;
Michael Meloony; John Emory.

1789 June Court
A-287 James Nicols re: RICHARDSON'S CHOICE
   Com: Peter Edmondson, Thomas Wynn Loockerman, William Frazier, John
Mitchell
   Nathaniel Warrington, DOR, 53 years(1789) ment: John Richardson;
John Nicols; Rice Levenus.
   William Edmondson, 64 years(1789) ment: Alexander Frazier.
   Ellis Thomas, 33 years(1789) ment: Thomas Barrow; James Edmondson;
William Jones; John Richardson.
   Henry Edgell, 38 years(1789) ment: William Barrow; Lydia Nicols;
John Willis.

1790 March Court
A292- Christopher Pratt re: BRANFIELD
   Com: Henry Downes, Thomas Barrow, Charles Emory
   Thomas Hardcastle, 53 years(1789) ment: SAWYER'S ADDITION; Benjamin
Ensworth; Mary Ensworth; William Dinkle; Solomon Kenton. Taken in
presence of Samuel Martindale, Jacob Pratt, John and Robert Hard-
castle; Christopher Pratt; Joshua Chilcutt.

1789 June Court
A297-Isaac Boon re: BOON'S VENTURE, DEAD RIDGE, BOON'S PURCHASE
   Com: Thomas Mason, John Hardcastle, Charles Emory
   James Boon Sr., 44 years(1790) ment: HOGG POINT; William Boon Sr.
   Joseph Whitby Sr., 60 years(1790), Quaker, ment: Jacob Boon son of
James.

1786 June Court
A303-Peter Edmondson re: EDMONDSON REGULATION, TAYLORS RAMBLE, EDMOND-
SON'S CHANCE, EDMONDSON'S LUCK
    Com: Philip Walker, Stephen Fleharty, William Frazier, Joshua Willi
    Maccabees Alford, 53 years(1787) ment: James Waddell; William Has-
    kins; RETALIATION; William Stevens, dec'd.
    James Waddell, 56 years(1787).
    Henry Edgell, 36 years(1787).
    Richard Collison, 48 years(1787) ment: Francis Edmondson; Charles
    Blair.

1790 October Court
A311-John Ridue re: HICKORY RIDGE and BEAR POINT
    Com: Charles Emory, Thomas Mason, Benjamin Sylvester
    Joseph Whitby, 61 years(1790), Quaker ment: old Robert Elliott;
    Joseph James; John Bcon; James Toldson; old Jacob Boone; Absalom
    Chance; Benjamin Whitby; JAMES RESERVE.

A317-John Derochbrune, William Hooper, William Dulaney, Lemuel Wooters,
    Matthew Derochbrune and Henry Downes re: BETSEY'S or BETT'S RANGE,
    VAUGHN'S KINDNESS and LARGE RANGE.
    Com: Charles Emory, Thomas Penington, Neal Price.
    Ment: BAYNARDS LARGE RANGE ADDITION.

A324-John Stevens re: CHANCE'S DESIRE depends on DANBY
    Com: Zabdiel Potter, Thomas Barrow, Joseph Douglass
    William Stevens, Quaker, 56 years(1790) ment: his bro, John Stevens;
    Thomas White, Elijah Williamson.
    Thomas White, KENT CC DEL, 61 years(1790) ment: James Smith; Robert
    Bishop; _____ Bell.
    Levin Smith, 38 years(1790) ment: his father, James Smith.
    Jessey Grayless, 52 years(1790) ment: William Rich; John Stevens
    Bell.
    Noted that Mr. Thomas Barrow, commissioner, was dec'd.
    Also ment: George Martin, John Salsbury, Balaam Stafford, Henry
    Swiggett.

1791 March Court
A-334-John Fisher of Q.A. and Benjamin Blunt of CAR re: CODDS HEAD MANOR
    Com: Henry Thomas, Thomas Hughlett, Charles Emory, Thomas Barrow
    Thomas Baggs, 81 years(1790) ment: his father, John Baggs; Richard
    Harrington; Thomas Fisher; OLD TOWNE; John Swift.

A339-Above case continued:
    Com: Henry Downes; Thomas Hughlett, Charles Emory; William Whiteley,
    Thomas Barrow.
    Ment: POPLAR NECK, TAYLOR'S DESIRE, John Heney(?), Esq.; Joseph
    Fisher; William Starkey; Sarah Fisher; Flower Fisher; John Moffett;
    Clark Warren; William Tarbutton; Richard Harrington.

1792 March Court
A349-Lemuel Wright re: DRY SAVANNAH
    Com: Joseph Douglass, Joseph Nicols, Josiah Sterling, James Summers,
    Joshua Willis, Jr.
    Lewis Ross, 56 years(1790) ment: Thomas Barrow
    James Wright, son of Levin, 30 years, Quaker,(1790) ment: his father
    Also ment: Thomas Smith; Daniel Wright; Major Victors; James Wright;

14

Mary Wright, William Andrew.

1792 October Court
A355-James Boon re: HADDEN
Com: Philemon Downes, John Hardcastle, Jr., Robert Posthlewaite,
Ezekiel Hunter, 63 years(1792) ment: Dr. Kitturage; Capt. Knotts;
William Fairbanks; Isaac Boon; Joseph Boon; GARDEN OF ROSES.
Thomas Swan, 80 years(1792) ment: Thomas Fisher; James Boon; Francis Moore; Thomas Faulkner.
Joseph Whitby, 63 years(1792).

1793 March Court
A361-William Camper re: GRIFFITH'S PURCHASE
Com: Joseph Douglass, Joseph Nicols, Charles Emory
Rebecca Falkner, 36 years(1792) ment: SMALL PROFFIT; Thomas Falkner, her father.
John Lister, 40 years(1792).
Jacob Falkner, 33 years(1792) ment: Salathiel Falkner, his bro.
Thomas Lewis, 30 years(1792).

1793 October Court
A366-Philemon Downes and Elizabeth, his wife, re: BAYNARD'S CHANCE
Com: Robert Postlewhaite, Neal Price, John Dickinson, Thomas Pennington.
James Stewart, 21 years(1791) ment: Michael Maloney; REDFORD; JONE'S
FORREST; John Webb.
John Freeman, 31 years(1791) ment: Charles Daffin; Henry Martindale.
John Hardcastle of TA, 49 years(1791) ment: Bennett Morgan; Seth
and Nicols.
James Barwick, 56 years(1791) ment: his father, Edward Barwick;
Nowell's land.
Ment: Burton Falconer, David Barrow. Taken in presence of Robert
and Henry Hardcastle, William Steward, David D. Barrow, Levin Hicks,
Jacob Seth, Philip Casson.

A371-William Mason re: WINCHESTER'S FOLLY RESURVEYED
Com: Charles Emory, Samuel Jackson, Thomas Hardcastle
Also ment: Thomas Mason, STRATON, TILGHMAN'S GIFT, WINCHESTER'S
FOLLY.

1793 October Court
B1- John Mitchell, son of John Mitchell, dec'd, and his sister, Sarah
Mitchell re: MITCHELL'S DEFENSE
Com: George Martin, Zabdiel Potter, Thomas Loockerman, William
Richardson, Peter Edmondson.

B5- Benjamin Sylvester re: FISHER'S MEADOWS and AYLER'S FORTUNE
Com: Charles Emory, Neal Price, Jacob Pratt
James Knotts, 42 years(1790) ment: John Willson, John Ayler.
Richard Fisher, 56 years(1790) ment: Arthur Emory; his bro, Thomas
Fisher; Nathan Bradly.
John Longfellow, 50 years(1790) ment: James Fisher, Charles Bradley.

B11- Elizabeth Greensbury Ennells of DOR re: WILLINGSBOROUGH and EDMOND-
SON'S ADDITION
Com: William Richardson, Zabdiel Potter, Charles Blair, John Dickinson, Joseph Douglass.

15

William Frazier, 35 years(1792) ment: Charles Goldsborough; PLAIN
DEALING; Mr. Barrow; Mr. Richard Collison.
James Edmondson, Quaker, 55 years(1792) ment: Mr. William Ennells;
Alexander Frazier.
Andrew Banning, 64 years(1792) ment: Daniel Cheezum; Capt. Thomas
Noel; Zadoc Harvey.
Also ment: SHERWIN'S CHANCE, SKILLINGTON'S RIGHT, RICHARDSON'S
FOLLY, SKIPTON, RANGE, FRAZIER LOTT, SHERWIN'S FOLLY.

B18- Caleb Clark re: CLARK'S FANCY and CLARK'S CHANCE
John Waddell re: ADDITION to EDGELL'S LOT
Thomas ALcock re: OUT RANGE depends on CABIN RIDGE
Notices given to William Harrison, Brumwell Andrew, James Waddell,
Sr., Edward Smith, Owen Connally, Charles Blair, Levin Clark, Robert
Williams.
Com: William Frazier, Joshua Willis, William Robinson
David Woolford, 40 years(1793) ment: Walter Stevens, dec'd.
James Waddel, 62 years(1793).
Also ment: STEVEN'S BEGINNING.

B26- Nancy Wooters re: JUMP'S LANE
Notices given to: Eliza Hill, George Porter, Rachel Walker, John
Currey, James Casson, Jacob Pratt, Matthew Driver, William Gording.
Com: Henry Downes, John Green, George Martin
Benjamin Jump, 51 years(1794) ment: Thomas Jump; Thomas Beall.
Also ment: DUDLEY'S DESIRE, widow William's land called WILLIAMS
HAZARD.

1794 October Court
B29- Joseph Anthony re: PEARSON'S CHANCE
Com: George Martin, Robert Orrell, Thomas Hughlett
Robert Talboy, 35 years(1794) ment: Philip Horney; William Talboy.
John Woothers, 58 years(1794) ment: Jeffrey Horney; Betsey Pierson.
James Ewen, 60 years(1794) ment: William Seth; Thomas White.
John Scot, 62 years(1794) ment: Philemon Horney son of Jeffrey.
Mary Harris, Nicholite, 54 years(1794) ment: Thomas or John Lever-
ton, sons of John Leverton.
Also ment: William Carey, William Cahal.

B33- James Summers re: HAMSTED which James Ewing owns part of same.
Com: George Martin, Matthew Driver, Thomas Hughlett, Peter Edmond-
son, Charles Emory.
John Smith, Quaker, no age given(1780) ment: Patrick Quatermus;
Thomas Pearson, Dickinson's land.
John Saulsbury, no age given(1780).
James Dixon, 42 years(1793) ment: Thomas Barrow; Thomas White;
Joseph Foster; Felix Summers.
Thomas White, 63 years(1793) ment: John Saulsbury; Col. Lloyd.
John Allen Sangston, no age given(1793).
William Bishop, Quaker, 45 years(1795) ment: Anthony Willoughby;
DENBY; his father, Richard Willoughby.
John Richardson, New Quaker, 54 years(no date given) ment: Seth
Hill Evitts; William Rich; Jonathan Wilson.
Daniel Hignut, 49 years(1795).
Richard Sparks, 45 years(no date given) ment: John Allen Sangston;
Henry Swiggett; Edward Willoughby.
William Summers, 43 years(1795) ment: John Pearson.

16

B40- John Bennett re: MARTINDALE'S HOPE
      Com: Henry Downes, William Potter, Thomas Hughlett
      Notices to: Samuel Martindale, Jacob Pratt, Charles Pratt
      William Gording, 45 years(1794) ment: Thomas Pennington, Jacob Pratt

B43- Edward Bourke, Edward Bourke, Jr., Nathan Bourke and Elizabeth
      Bourke re: POPLAR RIDGE and POPLAR RIDGE ADDITION
      Com: Henry Downes, Philemon Downes, Francis Sellers, William
      Robinson, James Dwiggins.
      Notices to: William Colsent, Cloudsbery Cooper(tenant to Barrol),
      Jonathan Maloney (tenant to Corrie), James Dwiggins (tenant to
      Bryon, Thomas Wadman (tenant to Bryon), Jonathan Conner (tenant
      to Cooper), Solomon Wilson, James Wilson, James Kenton.
      John Ewin, 37 years(1794) ment: Solomon Kenton.
      Also ment: Felix Summers, Thomas Bourke, Mary Bourke, Sarah Bourke,
      JOHN'S CHANCE.

1791 October Court.
B46- James Edmondson re: RICHARDSON'S CHOICE depends on FOX HILL
      Com: Zabdiel Potter, Charles Blair, John Dickinson, Thomas Loock-
      erman, Severn Teackle.
      William Edmondson, Quaker, 67 or 68 years(1792) ment: Felix Sum-
      mers; Benjamin Nicols, William Edmondson, his uncle, Samuel Dickin-
      son, Benoni Frazier, Moses Walker.
      John Richardson, Nicolite, 52 years(1792) ment: Joseph Nicols,
      Charles Goldsborough, James Edmondson; his father, John Richardson,
      late of this county; Thomas Perry, dec'd; John Mitchell.
      William Jones, 61 years(1793) ment: Thomas Barrow; Rice Levenus;
      Elias Thomas, 36 years(1792) ment: his grandfather, John Richardson
      John Willis, 62 years(1793) ment: his father, John Willis, dec'd.
      James Nicols, 27 years (1794) ment: James Edmondson, John Willis,
      Philip Willis, Joshua Willis, Robert Thomas.
      Henry Edgell, 43 years(1794) ment: Lidia Nicols, mother of James
      Nicols; William Barrow.
      Edward Pinder Gollerthem, 47 years(1793) ment: John Sisk, Isaac
      Willis.
      John Willis, 62 years(1793) ment: RICHARDSON'S CHOICE; Rice Levenus;
      William Perry; Alexander Frazier; William Perry father of William
      Perry who lives in TA.
      Thomas Edmondson, Quaker, 53 years, no date given, KENT CO DEL,
      ment: Lidia Nicols, widow of John; William Askins, surveyor of DOR.

1795
B53- Howel Kenton and wife, Elizabeth; Henry Kenton and wife, Lydia;
      William Clark and wife, Mary; Joseph Kinnemont and wife, Margaret;
      and James, Henry, Nathan, Ann and Henrietta Downes, children of
      Aaron Downes,dec'd, re: MILFORD'S MITE and PARKE'S FRESHES.
      Com: Robert Hardcastle, Henry Hardcastle, William Chilton, Richard
      Oxenham, James Dwiggins, Jr.

1794
B56- Athel Stewart re: SYLVESTER'S FOREST
      Com: Henry Downes, Robert Hardcastle, George Martin
      Ment: John Bennett, Samuel Martindale.

1795
B58- Charles Lecompte re: DISCOVERY

Com: William Whitely, Thomas Hughlett, George Martin, Thomas Boon,
Richard Kennard.
Ment: Christopher Driver; Mrs. Driver; Thomas Lecompt; John White;
James Lecompt, Jr.

1796
B71- Thomas Valliant re: PINEY POINT and CLAYLAND, joint owner with
Matthias Alford, Jnth. Bozman, T. Vickers.
Notices to: Levin Blades, Thomas Wing, John Bozman, Matthias Al-
ford, Andrew Mitchell.
Com: William Frazier, William Needles, John Mitchell.
Ment: Joshua Willis, Jr., surveyor; John Fleharty and Hugh Hubbert,
chain carriers.

1795
B74- Joseph Rogers and Frances, his wife, the dau of John Smith, dec'd.,
who d January last(1795) re: WHEATLEY'S PARK. Smith left Frances
Rogers; James about 18 years; George about 13 years; Rachel about
7 years; Rebecca about 5 years; Ader about 3 years; Hannah about
18 mos. Levin Smith is guardian to minors.
Com: William Robinson, Robert and John Hardcastle, James Casson,
John Bennett.

1795
B77- Peter Taylor Causey and his wife, Elizabeth Causey; John Wilson,
taylor; Robert Causey and his wife, Margaret Causey re: William
Wilson who d Dec 1789 owning LLOYD'S REGULATION, SHADWELL, MT.
ANDREW. He left ELizabeth Causey; John Wilson; Robert Wilson
(over 20 yrs and under 21 yrs); James Wilson(over 19 years);
Deborah, wife of William Blake; Margaret(15 to 16 yrs); Ann about
14 yrs; Sarah about 12 yrs - Peter Causey guardian to last three
minors - all brothers and sisters to dec'd.
Com: George Martin, Peter Rich, John Mitchell, William Gibson,
Richard Sparks.

1796
B82- Abraham Lewis and Thomas Lewis, sons of Thomas Lewis, dec'd., re:
WORLD'S END.
Com: George Martin, Thomas Baynard, Levin Noble, John Mitchell,
William Potter.
Elijah Dean, 57 years(1797) ment: Joshua Chilcut; John Chilcut.
James Summers, 48 years(1797) ment: old Anthony Chilcut's descen-
dants who are John and Anthony Chilcut.
Edward Russum, 67 years(1797) ment: John Layton; Thomas Lewis.
Ment: Peter Harris, John Shepherd, John Layton, Jacob Faulkner.

1795
B86- Peter, Rachel, Ann, William andElizabeth Sharpe re: MT. PLEASURE
depends on BRANFIELD.
Com: James Casson, John Bennett, George Martin
Parrott Roe, 47 years(1797) ment: John Fisher, Henry Sharp.

1797
B88- Sally Swan; James Ryall and his wife, Betty; say Thomas Swan d
1796, owned BROUGHTEN. BROUGHTEN'S ADDITION, leaving above heirs
and Thomas Swan, a son; James and Arabella Swan, grandchildren,
minors.

Com: John Hardcastle, John Bennett, Thomas Bell, Henry Casson, Major Thomas Mason.

1797
B93- Charles Lecompte re: ADDITION TO DISCOVERY and SECOND DISCOVERY, the property of John White, Dr. Edward White, and Thomas and James Lecompte.
Com: William Whitely, Thomas Hughlett, George Martin, Peter Rich, Charles Jones.
Notices to: James Lecompte 3rd, Christopher Driver, Matthew Driver, Edward and John White.
James Lecompte, 70 years(1797)

1797
B96- Henry Porter, KENT, DEL, re: JUMP'S CHANCE, CHILTON'S LEVELL, NEW CUNNINGHAM - that John Porter, KENT, DEL, d 30 June 1795 and had ch: Henry Porter; Rebecca wife of Samuel Turner; Sarah wife of Abraham Jump; Ann Porter about 12 yrs; George Porter about 14 yrs; Mary Porter about 8 years.
Com: John Hardcastle, Samuel Talbot, Thomas Bell, Samuel Bell, William Hardcastle.

1796
B101-Thomas Goldsborough of Foster Goldsborough, TA, re: THE THREE BOUNDED HICKORYS, THE GOOSE POND depends on MURPHEY'S ADDITION.
Notices sent: James Dillen, Deborah Dickinson, Dr. S.T. Johnson, Thomas Daffin, Stanley Loockerman, John and James Dickinson, William Blades, Jacob Loockerman, William Andrew, Mary Blades, John Dawson, Elizabeth and Peter Eaton, Caleb Eaton, John Beauchamp, Elijah Carmean, and to tenants on the land, Nathan Manship, Joshua Hobbs, Robert Harding and Owen McQuality.
Com: John Bennett, Solomon Brown, George Martin.
Thomas Towers, 50 years(1797)
Joseph Richardson, 52 years(1797) ment: William Dawson
William Andrew, 55 years(1797).

1798
B105-Thomas Turner re: RIMOALD, BANK OF PLEASURE depends on PAINTER'S RANGE.
Com: John Mitchell, John Stevens, Joseph Nicols, William Frazier.
Joseph Bland, 80 years(1798) ment: William Spencer, dec'd.
Elijah Dean, 57 years(1798) ment: his father, Francis Dean; John Willis; Nathan Beatey; Henry Turner.
Ellis Thomas, 43 years(1798) ment: Isaac Willis and John Chipley, both dec'd; Capt. William Haskins.
James Andrew, 44 years(1798) ment: James Alexander.
Richard Andrew, 25 years(1798) ment: William Nicols; Jacob Charles; Peter Taylor of DOR.
Beachum Andrew, 46 years(1798) ment: James Dawson, William and Thomas Gray; George Andrew.
Nehemiah Andrew, 42 years(1798) ment: Richard Lane; Francis Dean; Joshua Dilling; William Collins; Solomon Hobbs.
Samuel Sparkland, 39 years(1798).
James Cohee, DOR, 52 years(1798) ment: Daniel Sulivane, John Willis the elder; Edward Dean; Charles Dickinson; John Sulivane; Thomas Turner; Jasper Wood.

Peter Edmondson, TA, 45 years(1798) ment: John Willis; William
Nicols; Edward Coursey; Samuel Earl.
Jarvis Willis, 63 years(1798) ment: Henry Turner father of Thomas
Turner.
Isaac Andrew, 57 years(1798) ment: his father John Andrew; John
Sullivane.
Edward Pinder Gollotherm, 51 years(1798) ment: Isaac and John
Willis.
James Murphey, DOR, Quaker, 57 years(1798) ment: Dorcas Nicols;
her brother, John Willis or Jonathan Willis.
Thomas Wynn Loockerman, 46 years(1798).
Joseph Billeter, 57 or 58 years(1798) ment: John Willis half-bro
of John Willis; Daniel Cromean.

1798
B114-Perry A. Sumption and his wife,Elizabeth; Richard Ridgaway and
his wife, Henrietta; William, John, Thomas, Sarah, Cecelia and
Rachel, sons and daus of Benjamin Townsend who died possessed of
WHITBEY'S HAZARD and IRISH DISCOVERY and DUBLIN - he d 17 January
1790.
Com: Thomas Hughlett Caleb Boyer, James Boon, William Coursey,
Thomas Mason.

1798
B119-Joseph Rogers re: WHEATLEY'S PARK states that John Smith d January
1795 leaving my wife. Frances Rogers, now dec'd, who had dau,
Elizabeth Rogers, also dec'd, and James, George, Rachel, Rebecca,
Ader and Hannah Smith, all infants.
Com: Robert, John and Henry Hardcastle, John Bennett, Solomon
Kenton.

1798
B123-John Hirem Dwigans pet that Ann Dwigans d 15 Sept 1794 owning
LYFORD which desc to John Hirem Dwigans, Bennett Dwigans, Ann
Dwigans and Rachel Webb, all sons and daus. Bennett and Ann
are minors.
Com: Joshua Clarke, Henry Downes, Henry Hardcastle, John Hard-
castle, Thomas Daffin.

1798
B126-John Mitchell re: ADVENTURE, LLOYD'S FOREST, COURSEY'S NEGLECT,
HARDSHIP now surveyed as MITCHELL'S DEFENSE.
Com: John Bennett, George Martin, Peter Harris.

1798
B129-Thomas Daffin, Francis Sellers, James and Giles Hicks re:
DAFFIN'S FARM, MILFORD, PARKER'S FRESHES, GREEN CLOSE, CHANCE
and HICK'S PLAINS.
Notices to: David Webber(tenant to Arthur Bryan), Joshua Cooper,
Henry Martindale, William Shehan, Sarah Catrop, Daniel Catrop,
Thomas Hicks, Elizabeth Oxenham, William Burton(tenant to John
Corrie's heirs).
Com: John Fisher, George Martin, Henry Hardcastle.
Samuel Kinnemon, 49 years(1799) ment: Benjamin Anthony, Mr.
Bozman, Mrs. Webb, Charles Daffin, Aaron Downes, Hawkins Downes.
Robert Jones, Q.A., 45 years(1799).
Cloudsbery Cooper, 47 years(1799) ment: THE BEGINNING.

William Gordon, 46 years(1799) ment: James Curtis
Isaiah Medes, 58 years (1799 ment: Thomas Medes
William Burton, 65 years(1799) ment: Edward Cahall, Thomas W. Medes,
James Dwigans, Michael Smith and Holiday's land.
Charles Critchett, 38 years(1799) ment: Thomas Barrow.
John Freeman(of TA) 38 years(1799)
Thomas Whittington Medes, 37 years(ot TA) (1799) ment: Sharpless
Cooper.
William Oxenham, 20 years(1799) ment: James Bell, TURNER'S PLAINS
ADDITION.
Henry Hardcastle of TA, 33 years(1799) ment: Henry Holladay, Thomas
Eagle, and his father, Solomon Eagle.
William Burton, 64 years(1799) ment: Aaron Downes son of Hawkins
Downes; Vincent Price.
Also ment: Thomas Golt and heirs of Abner Clements.

1799
B139-William Wilson re: CONTROVERSY
Notices to: George Martin, Joshua Cooper, Joshua Cranor, Robert
Williams guardian to minor named Skinner; Mrs. Elizabeth Over-
stocks.
Com: John Mitchell, Peter Harris, Solomon Cooper.
Emory Craynor, 35 years(1800) ment: Henry Ward.
Solomon Kent, Quaker, 50 years(1800).
John Morgan, KENT DEL, 40 years(1800) ment: James Smith of WHEAT-
LEY'S PARK who raised John Morgan; Daniel Skinner; William Wilson;
Reuben Allen.
Benjamin McNiece, 45 years(1800) ment: Emanuel Craynor, Solomon
Wright.
Levin Smith, 50 years(1800) ment: John Smith, James Smith.
John Willson, Jr. 25 years(1800), Quaker, ment: Joseph Porter.
James Willson, Jr. 30 years(1800), Quaker.
Mary Coldscut, KENT DEL, 66 years(1800) ment: Robert and Greens-
bury Goldsborough.
Elenor Smith wid of John, 40 years(1800).

1800
B145-Samuel Andrew d seized of ANDREW'S FORTUNE and MOORE'S CASTLE
leaving Thomas; Elizabeth; Sarah wife of Jeremiah Dukes; Nancy;
Esther; Samuel; Margaret; Nimrod Andrew (last three minors).
Com: Thomas Nicols, William Potter, Seth H.Evitts, Shadrack
Lighton, Peter Harriss.

1800
B149-Thomas Alcock d 1796 owned OUTRANGE, ADDITION TO ALCOCK'S LOTT,
MISCHANCE, ALCOCKS CHANCE, BILLETER'S LANDING, BURTONWOOD'S
NEGLECT, LLOYD'S KINDNESS, MILL LAND, PARTNERSHIP IN FISHING
PLEASANT RED OAK POND, and lands bought of John Dawson with no
name. He left three sisters and two dec'd sisters' children:
Elizabeth Alcock; Nancy Alcock and Catherine Green(formerly
Alcock); Thomas, and James Buchanan and William Green, ch of
dec'd sis, Sarah, who m Thomas Buchanan, then Jesse Green;
Philip Woolford, son of sis, Joanna, who m David Woolford.
Com: Solomon Brown, William Potter , John Young, Peter Harriss,
John Mitchell.

1803
B155-Phil Harrington re: FISHER'S CHANCE.
    Com: Thomas and Robert Hardcastle, James Pearce.
    James Brodey, 40 years(1803) ment: Thomas Baggs; Anthony Cox;
    Richard Harrington; John Millis eldest son of John Millis.
    Thomas Brodey, 30 years(1803).

1802
B158-John Voss Baker d 15 April 1790 seized of HOBBS FOLLY, CLAY SWAMP,
    ADDITION TO CLAY SWAMP leaving John of age; Thomas of age; Mary;
    Esther; Benjamin, minors; and Ann wife of Elijah Chance, of age.
    Com: William Potter, John Mitchell, Seth H. Evitts, John Stanton,
    Elijah Satterfield.

1801
B162-Govert Haskins pet for roadway to HASKINS LANDING and ADDITION TO
    HASKINS LANDING.
    Ment: heirs of Levin Blades, Richard Willoughby, heirs of William
    Willoughby, John Billeter, Thomas Valient.

1803
B164-William Emerson purchased right of George Spurrey, son of John
    Spurrey who d March 1793 seized of SHADWELL and LLOYD'S REGULATION.
    Left George, eldest son over 21; Sally Emory under 21; William
    and Elizabeth Spurrey, who are minors.
    Com: John Bennett, Robert Orrell, Benjamin Denny, William Summers,
    William Carey.
    Ment: Clousberry Williamson and Mark Anthony appointed chain
    carriers for Robert Orrell, surveyor.
    John Spurrey left wife, Elizabeth, and her children: John Hobbs;
    Ann Hobbs and Elizabeth Hobbs, ch by her former husband. Solomon
    Rouse m Elizabeth Hobbs. Ann Hobbs is dec'd. William Kirkman
    m John Spurrey's widow.
    Ment: Thomas Boon, John Cooper.

1803
B169-Samuel Culbreth re: POPLAR NECK
    Com: Robert Orrell, Thomas Hardcastle, George Martin
    Ment: John Fisher

1803
B171-William Webb re: LYFORD originally granted to George Yates,Jr.
    1000 acres in 1666. Adjoins SEWELL'S RANGE.
    Com: Henry Downes, Henry Nicols, George Martin
    Robert Jadwin, KENT DEL, 60 years(1804) ment: John Dwigins, James
    Dwigins, Solomon Ewell.

1805
B175-Richard Fisher, Jr. d 1794 without a will, seized with FISHER'S
    MEADOWS. Heirs are John Fisher over 21; William Fisher over 21;
    Lydia Blunt over 21, wife of Levi Blunt; Elizabeth Teat over 21;
    Rachel Fisher over 21; Esther Fisher under 21; Susannah Fisher
    under 21.
    Com: Alemby Jump, George Martin, John Jump, John Boon, Nathan
    Whitby.

1804
B178-Martin and William Norris re: BEETREE CORRECTED
        Com: Robert Orrell, Marcey Fountain, Thomas Clendening.
        Ment: Richard Hughlett guardian to Thomas Mason heirs; Major
        Thomas Mason; Philemon Spencer, William L. Weems, Samuel Martin-
        dale; FALCOME'S HOPE.

1804
B183-James Brodey and Philemon Harrington to ditch and drain their land.
        Com: Thomas Hardcastle, James Pearce, Thomas Mason, Richard Keene,
        Robert Hardcastle, Jr.
        Ment: Samuel Harrington.

1805
B188-Thomas Clendening and ELisha Burr re: BURTT'S FANCY ADDITION
        adj HOBBS VENTURE, KILL MADIN, JADWINS HAZZARD
        Com: Robert Orrell, Marcy Fountain, James Pearce.
        Ment: BUCK or BURTS RANGE; Henry Burtt, Eli Burtt, Elsberry Burtt.
        Chain carriers: Benjamin Pippin, Joseph Meredith.

1806
B196-James Barwick d seized of JUMP'S CHOICE, FISHER'S PLAINS, ROE'S
        FANCY. Ch: Edward, James, John, Rebecca, Letitia, Joshua, Ann
        and Mary Barwick who m John Thawley. Ann, Rebecca, Joshua and
        Mary are minors.
        Com: John Hardcastle, Samuel Talbot, Dekar Thompson, Daniel Bell,
        John Williams.
        Ment: John Fisher, Joseph Porter, and that John Barwick a res in
        PA.

1806
B203-Henry Willis d 1 Nov 1793 seized of PAINTER'S RANGE which desc.
        to Henry Willis, Levin Willis, and Elenor wife of John Gwinn of
        QA. Henry and Levin are infants.
        Com: William Frazier, Frederick Holbrook, William Haskins, John
        Keene, Thomas Wing.
        Land purchased by Jesse Connelly.

1806
B206 Peter Hardcastle to open a road to his farm. Ment: John Council.

1807
B208 John Deroachbrune d seized of VAUGHAN'S KINDNESS, left Ann wife
        of Henry Martindale; Jacob; Philemon; Peregrine and Sarah Deroach-
        brune, his children, last four infants.
        Com: Henry Downes, Henry Nicols, John Ruth, John Tillotson, Henry
        Kenton.

1806
B212 Ann Caldwell d 15 Feb 1806 seized of BAKER'S PLAINS and HUGHLETT'S
        ESCHEAT (one of heirs of Thomas Hughlett), she left two bros.,
        William and Richard Hughlett and a sis, Mary, wife of Charles
        Adams.
        Com: John Hardcastle, Batchelor Chance, William B. Keene, Joseph
        Hurd, Henry Coursey.
        ment: Cooper Kinderdine, Col. William Whiteley.

1807
B217-Mary Willson, Richarc A. Willson, Thomas Willson re: SEWELL'S
RANGE.
Com: Henry Downes, John Tilotson, Thomas Daffin, John Ruth, Henry
Nicols 3rd.
William Summers, 47 years(1808)
Philemon Plummer, 45 years(1808)

1808
B222-John Genn d leaving ch: Nathan, Elizabeth wife of Robert Jarmon,
Thomas of age, and William, Nancy and John who are minors, and
one grandchild, Margaret Genn, dau of an elder son now dec'd.
Re: MERRICKS DELIGHT, BANKS DELIGHT, BANKS ADDITION
Com: Nathan Whitby, Robert Hardcastle, Isaac Chance, Jonah Genn,
John Leath.

1806
B225-John Stevens d intestate since 5 Oct 1802 leaving grandchildren
as heirs at law: Nancy Stevens; John Stevens; Peggy Stevens m
William Corrie; Mary Stevens m John Johnson; Nancy Dean heir-at-
law of Elizabeth who m Solomon Dean; Horatio Stevens under 21,
has guardian Azel Stevens.
RE: STEVENS PURCHASE, STEVENS REST and CHANCE'S DESIRE.
Com: John Mitchell, William Potter, Frederick Holbrook, Solomon
Brown, John Keene.
New com: William Potter, Solomon Brown, George Collins, Elijah
Satterfield, James Grayless.
Ment: Robert and Alexander Polk, Thomas Stack, HARD FORTUNE and
DANBY.

1807
B231-James Clements re: HOBBS VENTURE
Com: Marcey Fountain, Henry Whiteley, Samuel Culbreth
John McCombs, 45 years(1807)

1808
B235-Joseph Hurd c 6 Dec 1307 seized of GOLDEN GROVE, HARDSHIP, ADDTN
TO HARDSHIP, MAIDENS FORREST, EXCHANGE, WHITESBOROUGH DIVIDED,
PARTNERSHIP(orig called LOOCKERMAN'S PURCHASE). Left four ch:
Major Hurd, Araminta wife of James Rich, William Hurd and Robert
Hurd, last two minors, and Mary Hurd, widow. William Whiteley
apptd guardian.
Com: William Hughlett, Charles Jones, Robert Bell, John Carter,
Marcey Fountain.

1808
B240-Nathaniel Fountain d 10 Mar 1803 seized of FANCY, POTTER'S PLAINS,
BROTHERHOOD. Left two daus: Ann wife of Anderton Fountain and
Kitturah Fountain a minor.
Com: John Young, Elijah Satterfield, Levi Dukes, James Grayless,
Frederick Holbrook.
Ment: DUNCASTER, Solomon Cranor, EDMONDSON'S RESERVE, Nathaniel
Potter, William Potter, Alexander Griffith.

1806
B244-James Reed d seized of NEW NOTTINGHAM RECTIFIED leaving ch:
William Reed, Elizabeth Reed, James Reed, Thomas Reed and Daniel
Reed(last four minors), with Henry Downes as guardian.

Com: Peregrine F. Bayard, John Hardcastle, Samuel Talbot, Alemby Jump, Charles Adams.
Ment: NEW BUCKBY

1808
B248-Richard Keene re: EDENBOROUGH
Com: Robert Hardcastle, James Pearce, Thomas Brodey, Samuel Harper, William Norris.
Chain carriers: Richard Williams and John Neal; surveyor, Marcy Fountain.
Ment: MANGY PORKEY
Gallant Lemare, 33 years(1808).

1809
B253-Jeremiah Rhodes re: MORGAN'S HAY LAND
Com: James Byrn, Frederick Holbrook, William Councill, Anthony Ross, Jr.
Ment: John Dillen, dec'd; James Stevens and wife.
Christopher Smith, 23 years(1809) ment: his father, Thomas Smith of Ralph Smith, dec'd.
Mary Stevens wife of James, 40 years(1809) ment: her father, John Dillen, dec'd, and her mother, Ann Dillen, dec'd.
John B. Smith, 25 years(1809) ment: his father, Thomas Smith.

1811
B256-James Boon re PARTNERSHIP
Com: Robert Orrell, Marcy Fountain, Nathan Whitby
John H.Faulkner and Thomas Bartlett, chain carriers for William Orrell, surveyor.
Ment: William Boon, Jacob Boon, OAK RIDGE, the late Tilghman Chance's heirs.

1810
B261-Thomas Brodey re: OAK RIDGE, GARDEN OF ROSES
Com: Robert Orrell, Marcy Fountain, Nathan Whitby
Ment: COOL SPRING
Daniel Bartlett, 20 years(1810) ment: "young" William Saulsbury
William Baulkner, 43 years(1810) ment: Tilghman Chance.
Major Nehemiah Townsend, 44 years(1810).
Christopher Willson, Quaker, 65 years(1810).
Bachelor Chance, 48 years, Quaker(1810) ment: Richard Chance and Dorrington Chance, now dec'd.

1810
B268-James Boon, minor under guardianship of John Boon re: PARTNER-SHIP and part of OAK RIDGE.
Com: Robert Orrell, Marcy Fountain, Nathan Whitby
Ment: heirs of TilghmanChance; Thomas Broadey; JAMES RESERVE; BOON'S PARK, HADDEN.

1810
B273 Isaac Purnell re: WHITE HALL (BEAR GARDEN resurveyed)
Com: John Boon, Nathan Whitby, William Chilton, Nathaniel Talbot.
Purnell Sylvester, 56 years(1810) ment: Valentine Green; William Whitby; BEAR GARDEN; his father, David Sylvester, dec'd.

1810
B275 Isaac Purnell re: DICKINSON'S PLAINS

Com: John Boon, Nathan Whitby, William Chilton, Nathaniel Talbot.
William Sylvester, 57 years(1810) ment: Benjamin Sylvester, Charles
Emory.
Solomon Cannon, 52 years(1810) ment: Thomas Barrow, Henry Dickinson
Thomas Sylvester, 29 years(1810).
Purnell Sylvester, 56 years(1810) ment: George Martin; old Joseph
Boon, John Malcom, both dec'd; GRUBBY NECK, GRUBBY NECK ADDTN;
John Elliott.

1808
B278-Peregrine F. Bayard guardian of Edward B. Hardcastle, son of Aaron
Hardcastle pet for outlet road.
Ment: William Tolson, heirs of James Bartlett, Thomas Hardcastle.

1809
B280-Frederick Holbrook re: DUNCASTER -also pet by William Dukes, Elijah
Satterfield, Thomas Bechamp, Bechamp Sarton, John Beachamp.
Com: William Potter, Massey Fountain, Stephen Lucas.
Chain carriers: Charles Ireland, James Harding, also James Johnson,
Levin Dein(?).
Levin Tull, 48 years(1809)
Abel Griffith, 35 years(1809) ment: William Fountain, Peter Colliso
John Warren, 39 years(1809).
John Harvey, 46 years(1809)
Linsey O.Breeding, 60 years(1809) ment: Richard F. Arlis
Abraham Collins Sr., 66 years(1809)
William Chaffinch, 29 years(1809)
Roger Fountain, 50 years(1809)

1809
B286-Levi Dukes and James Hubbard, whereas Philip Woolford d seized of
PLEASANT, NO NAME, ALCOCK'S FANCY, RED OAK POND leaving Ann wife
of Levi Dukes; Elizabeth wife of Thomas Hicks who was aunt of
Philip Woolford; Catharine wife of Robert Green, another aunt
and James and Thomas Buchanan and WilliamW. Green, sons of Sally
Green wife of Jesse Green, another aunt.
Com: William Potter, Peter Harris, Elisha Chaffinch, Edward
Barton, Willis Charles.
Ment: PETER'S PURCHASE, HERRFORD.

1811
B292-John Boon re: CO-PARTNERSHIP
Com: Marcy Fountain, Batchelder Chance, William Coursey.
William Orrell, survey; Thomas Bartlett and Garrison Matthews,
chain carriers.
Ment: Moses Boon, Isaac Purnell.
Moses Boon, 40 years(1811) ment: Joseph Whitby, dec'd; John Tolson,
dec'd; Blunt's land; his father, Moses Boon, dec'd.
James Boon, Sr., Quaker, 51 years(1811) ment: his father, William
Boon.
Nathan Whitby, 37 years(1811) ment: his father, Joseph Whitby, dec'
Thomas Bartlett, 46 years(1811) ment: Isaac Boon, dec'd.

1809
B298-Charles Ross pet that William Ross d intestate seized of land in
deed from Isaac Smith son of Levin, and Mary Smith, his wife, in
1795. William Ross left ch: Charles Ross; Edward Ross who is d

26

and left Anna, Charles and Mitchel Ross; Gibson Ross the son of
William Ross, dec'd; Anne Truitt, his dau who m John Truitt and
is now d leaving her husband and one dau, Eliza Truitt; Nathaniel
Ross, son of William, dec'd; Caleb Ross, his son; William Ross,
his son; and Daniel Ross, his son, a minor.
Com: Edward Hubbard, George Collins, Jacob Wright, Abraham Collins,
Peter T. Causey.
New com: Frederick Holbrook, George Collins, Abraham Collins, Peter
T. Causey, Cain Ross.

1808
B306 John Dawson of John of Fork Dist. pet that Nicholas Stubbs d 10
Feb 1801 seized of ADDTN TO TIMBER TREE NECK, LEVIN'S FOLLY EN-
LARGED, ADDTN TO MILES SWAMP leaving six ch: William, John, Mary,
Ann, Ealy and Richard Stubbs. All minors except William. Levin
Wright of Levin, Charles and Nancy Stubbs guardians to minors.
Com: Thomas H. Douglass, Jessee Cannon, Hatfield Wright, Noah
Dawson, Thomas Saulsbury.
Ment: Sovren Dawson.

1809
B313-Johnson Swiggett re: outlet road.
Ment: Lindsy O.Breeding, William Potter, William Swiggett, heirs
of Nathaniel Stafford, PUNCH HALL.

1810
B315-Thomas Alcock d 1796 seized of OUTRANGE, ALLCOCK'S FANCY, RED OAK
POND, NO NAME and PLEASANT. Lands awarded to James and Thomas
Buchanan and William W. Green.
Ment: Philip Woolford who do 1806; Levi Dukes.
Com: Peter Harris of TA, William Potter, Willis Charles, Fred
Holbrook,Anthony Ross, Jr.

1811
B320-Robert Jarman re: MERRICK'S DELIGHT
Com: William Orrell, Nathan Whitby, William Monticue, David Genn.
Richard Roe, 33 years(1811) ment: Greenbury Matthews, dec'd; Col.
Peter Rich.
Abner Roe, 29 years(1811).

1812
B323-Joseph Boon re: BOON'S PLEASURE
Com: Marcey Fountain, Nathan Whitby, William Coursey, Robert
Orrell, George Reed.
Ment: DICKINSON'S PLAINS, Benjamin Sylvester's heirs.
William Coursey, 52 years(1812) ment: Hinson Satterfield, Purnell
Sylvester, dec'd.

1811
B327-John Boon, Elizabeth Boon, Hawkins H. Boon by John Boon, their
guardian, re: DEAD RIDGE.
Com: Robert Orrell, Marcy Fountain, WilliamCoursey.
Chain carriers: Peter Sharp,Garrison Matthews.
Nathan Whitby, 38 years(1812) ment: his father, Joseph Whitby, dec'd

1812
B331-Levin Johnson d 1 Sept 1808 leaving ch: Margaret m Eli Connelly;

Charlotte m Nathan Grayless; Tilghman and Henry Johnson, minors.
Possessed of JOHNSON S DELIGHT, JOHNSON'S ENTRANCE, HARDSHIP.
Com: Charles Ireland, John Prouse, William Dukes, George A. Smith,
Elijah Satterfield.

1812
B334-Batchelor Chance re: BOON'S HAZARD depends on BANKS ADDITION.
Com: Robert Orrell, Seth Godwin, John Boon.
Ment: Isaac Purnel, Robert Fountain
Chain carriers: Charles Rouse, James Fountain.

1811
B337-Thomas Sylvester pet that Purnell Sylvester, his father, d intes-
tate on 14 May 1811, seized of GRUBBY NECK and GRUBBY NECK ADDTN.
Heirs: David of age; Nancy m Richard Legg, of age; Thomas of age;
Daniel about 18 yrs; Samuel about 14 yrs; Margaret about 14 yrs;
Sarah about 7 yrs.
Com: Joseph Boon, John Boon, William Chilton, William Parrott,
Samuel Talbott.

1812
B341-Thomas Roe d about 1798 seized of LANE'S RIDGE leaving ch: Wil-
liam; Rebecca wife of William Caperoon; Mary wife of James Cald-
well; Ann Roe; Jane Roe; Sarah Roe (last three minors)
Com: Selby Bell, Alenby Jump, Joseph Talbott, Job Williams,
William Chilton.

1814
B344-William Hughlett re: BYRNE'S PLAINS, DEER SKIN RIDGE, LAST VACANCY,
DENTON'S VALLEY, FORREST PLAINS, BEE TREE SWAMP.
Com: Marcy Fountain, Samuel Culbreth, Seth Godwin,
Chain carriers: Samuel LeCompte, William Martindale
Lewis Draper, 48 years(1814) ment: his father, Judril Draper;
his bro, Ephriam Draper.
William Gibson, 45 years(1814).
Solomon Pippin, 51 years(1814) ment: Joseph Pippin, dec'd; Robert
Davis; John Pippin, both dec'd.
John Cooper, KENT DEL, 49 years(1814) ment: Absalum Willoughby,
dec'd.
Robert Orrell, 53 years(1814) ment: George Martin, Joseph Hurd,
BATCHELDER'S CHANCE, Allen Wilson, Isaac Henry, John and Jenkins
Henry.
Ment: DOCTOR'S FANCY, White Turpin.
Chain carriers: Derias Pippin, Daniel Sylvester on FORREST PLAINS
survey.

1815
B354-James LeCompte and his wife, Elizabeth, who is heir of Thomas
LeCompte, late Car, d 1812 intestate owned LECOMPTE'S REGULATION,
left Elizabeth over 21 m James Lecompte; Fanny almost 21 m Joseph
Bell; Sarah over 21 and single; Priscilla under 21, single, whose
guardian is Joshua Driver.
Com: Robert Orrell, William Orell, Matthew Driver, Henry Driver,
Edward Carter.

1814
B357-Thomas Roe d 1799 owned LLOYD'S REGULATION leaving William,

28

Samuel, Thomas, John, Deborah and Abner, the last two minors.
Com: John Carter, Dennis Kelley, Thomas Pearson, James Keene,
Elijah Barwick.

1814
B360-William Virdin d owned MT. ANDREW leaving Margarett wife of
John Saulsbury; Moses Virdin; Elizabeth Virdin; Ruth wife of
John Clarke.
Com: William Potter, John Young, Thomas Styll, Alexander Maxwell,
Jenifer S. Taylor.

1813
B361-William Gray re: PAINTER'S MISTAKE
Com: William Potter, Elijah Satterfield, Elisha Dawson, Levi
Dukes, William McDonald.

1814
B364-Mary Adams, dec'd, wife of Charles Adams, also dec'd. She d
10 March 1808, seized of BAKER'S PLAINS and part of HUGHLETT'S
ESCHEAT, leaving ch: William H., Thomas, Charlotte, Sarah, Elenor
and Charles Adams. Charles Sr. d 10 Oct 1810. Charlotte d on
or about 10 Oct 1811. Thomas, Sarah, Elinor are minors.

1815
C1 -Emory Craynor d seized of CONTROVERSEY in 1813, left Emanuel
Craynor and Mary the wife of Henry Collins.

1815
C4 -Andrew Jump of TA, d 1811 seized of HORSE PASTURE, JUMP's LOT,
RICHARD & MARY'S FOREST, WILLIAMS NEGLECT.
He left William Jump; ELizabeth wife of Isaac Morgan and Sarah
Latchum; Nodera Latchum; Eliza Ann Latchum; Maria Latchum and
Winlock Latchum the ch of Margaret Latchum(formerly Margaret
Jump) the wife of Kendall Latchum; Allemby Jump purchased William
Jump's part.

1815
C8 -Henrietta Bozman d Nov 1801 without a will seized in part of
ALFORD'S FORTUNE, MILL'S HOPE, LOOCKERMAN'S BEGINNING. Lands
desc to Philemon Bozman over 21 yrs; George Bozman over 21 yrs;
Maccabees Bozman over 21 yrs; John Bozman over 21 yrs. and Eliza-
beth Bozman under 21 yrs; Lucretia Bozman under 21 yrs.

1815
C11 -Charles Manship d 1812 seized of REVIVAL and PERRY's GROVE.
Heirs are Mary Manship m Abraham Griffith; Maria who m Samuel
Lucas and Elizabeth Manship under 21 yrs. Widow, Ann, now
m to Samuel Talbott.

1815
C17 -Isaac Nicols d 1810 seized of THE GROVE, PLAIN DEALING, BARTLETT'S
MEADOWS leaving Edward Nicols; William Nicols; Rebecca wife of John
Handy; Tilghman Nicols; Mary Nicols and Washington Nicols(last
three minors).

1815
C21 -Vinson Dillen d March 1806 seized of LLOYDS GROVE. His widow,

29

now m to Pritchard Hudson(Richard Hudson). Dillen left ch:
John; Mark about 20 years; Ann who m Joseph Compton, now about
18 yrs and Mary Dillen who is 15 yrs.

1815
C24 -Anthony Banning of TA re: BANNING'S RETREAT formerly POWELL'S
VENTURE depends on DOCKERAY'S MEADOWS.

1815
C26 -William Cahall d 1812 seized of MAIDEN'S FORREST leaving ch:
John, eldest, of age; Esther of age; Winnafred; Solomon; Noah;
Elizabeth and Mary Cahall (last five infants).

1816
C29 -John Allen Sangston d 1 Dec 1802 leaving widow, Rachel, and ch:
Elizabeth wife of Alexander Maxwell, Jr.; Susan wife of Solomon
Wright; James and Allen(a minor) and gr-ch: John, Thomas, Henry,
Eliza wife of William Whiteley; Mary wife of Samuel Slaughter,
all born of Rebecca Baynard, dau of John Allen Sangston, who d
before him.

1816
C32 -Thomas Roe d 29 January 1807, intestate, seized of ABNER'S PARK,
WOOTERS CHOICE Resurveyed, SUSANNA'S RIGHT leaving widow, Mary
Roe and ch: Thomas; Arn m Samuel Matthews; Mary m David Sylvester;
Rebecca m Parrott Roe; Sarah m Levi Chance; Elizabeth, minor
between 15 or 16 yrs; James Roe, a minor about 14 yrs.
Ment: John Turner, James Clements and his wife, Ann Clements.

1816
C36 -James Roe, the elder, d Sept 1789 seized of ROE'S ADDITION.
Ch: Elizabeth Baggs; David; Sarah wife of Samuel Milburn; Marga-
ret wife of Joel Clements; Parrott; Ann wife of Peter Wilson;
Samuel and James Roe. David d May 1815 leaving Wilson; James;
Sarah and Elizabeth Roe, minors, under guardian Thomas Mason.

1816
C39 -Thomas Redden, DEL, pet that William Alford d seized with
ALFORD'S FORTUNE, leaving William, Ann, Mary and James Alford.
Ann is now dec'd having m James Colston, leaves one dau,
Eliza Ann Colston, a minor. Mary and James Alford are minors.

1816
C43 -Matthew Smith d May 1801 seized of KIRKHAM'S DISCOVERY. His
widow is since dec'd - ch: Charles Smith recently arrived at
21, Ann Smith and Eliza Smith, who are minors.

1816
C46 -Isaac Nicols is dec'd, owned land and sawmill, descended to
Rebecca wife of John Handy; Edward and William Nicols of full
age; and to Tilghman, Mary, and Washington Nicols, infants.

1817
C50 -Robert Walker d 1st May 1810 leaving Mahala m John Thomas;
Henry and Valiant Walker of age; Kitty, Mariah, who are infants.
Owned SARAH'S DELIGHT, EDMONDSON'S PURCHASE, FRAZIER'S LOT,
PERRY'S FLINTSHIRE alias PERRY'S DESIRE. William Dillon, guardian
to minors. Joseph Fleharty purchased some rights to land.

1817
C52 -Beacham Causey d 1802 leaving wid who has since d and ch: Eliza-
beth, Robert, Curtis, Eleanor, Beachamp, Nancy wid of William
Jester and Ann Causey. Eliza m Asa Dawson; Robert Causey d
leaving dau, Eliza who m Samuel Long, of TA, and is about 19 yrs.
Eleanor m Andrew Reed of TA.

1816
C56 -William Wheeler d 4 March 1812 leaving ch: Ann wife of Edward
Pritchett, of age; Mahal Wheeler about 18 yrs; the petitioner,
Thomas Wheeler, and Rebecca Wheeler, by their guardian George
W. Collison. William Wheeler owned INCLSOURE, PETER'S EXCEP-
TIBLE LOT, HABBAKUK'S ADDTN or MORGANS ADDTN, MARRATT'S LOT,
MARRATT'S MISTAKE or BIRCH GROVE.

1817
C64 -Thomas Stack d 22 Nov 1814 leaving three sons: Levin, Peter and
John, last two infants. Stack owned HARRY'S SETTLEMENT ENLARGED,
OUTRANGE and WILTSHIRE.

1817
C68 -Henry Jump petitions for new road.

1818
C69 -James McQuality d June 1806 leaving wid, Margaret, and ch: Joseph,
Catharine and Elizabeth. Catharine of age is m to Bennett Tomlin-
son of TA. Elizabeth, a minor, lives in TA. Widow, Margaret, m
David Fountain. McQuality owned HARRIS'ES OUTLET, VAUX'S ADDTN,
FRIENDSHIP REGULATED.

1818
C77 -Thomas Edgell petitions re: THE LOT

1818
C80 -Benjamin Sylvester d 17 March 1795 leaving dau, Martha, and gr-ch:
Serena and Clarissa Purnell, daus of Isaac Purnell of BALTO, dec'd.
Martha also had, Frederick, Adeline and Mary Purnell, and died
15 June 1805. Serena m Edmond Pendleton and had: Isaac Purnell
Pendleton and Serena Catherine Pendleton and has since d. Isaac
Purnell d 11 Aug 1813. Benjamin Sylvester owned WHITE HALL, WILL-
INLE, CARMARTHEAN, GRUBBY NECK, GRUBBY NECK ADDTN, BUCK RANGE,
BITE THE BITER, SELF DEFENSE, CHANCE, FARMER'S FIELDS, BOON'S PLEA-
SURE, BOON'S COURT, COMMON SENSE DISCOVERED, adj PARTNERSHIP, CO-
PARTNERSHIP, SATERFIELD'S LUCK, DICKINSON'S PLAINS, MALCOLM'S FARM,
SPRING FIELD, ABNER'S PARK, TILGHMAN'S GIFT, SCOTT'S FRIENDSHIP,
GREENFIELD, GLANDING'S BEGINNING, AYLER'S FORTUNE, THE SECTOR REC-
TIFIED, JUMP'S LOT, HUNTER'S HAZARD, SCARBOROUGH, CHESTNUT RIDGE,
THE DISCOVERY, SYLVESTER'S PARK, FISHER'S MEADOWS, STORY'S PARK,
CHILTON'S ADVENTURE, FARMER'S LOT, FARMER'S CHANCE ADDTN, TOULSON'S
DESIRE, HAZZARD, SYLVESTER'S STRINGLE.

1816
C109-Richard Ward, DEL, D 15 Oct 1812, owned GREEN'S PROJECT. Heirs
were Henry Ward, idiot and bro; Mary, sis and wid of Levin Wright;
Daniel Wright and Mary Wright ch of Ann Wright, a dec'd sis; Mary
Wright hath d and left Peter Wright and Rachel Wright(un 21) and a
sister, Rachel Kelly wife of William Kelly; James Ward a bro now

dec'd leaving son, Daniel, a minor; and Lydia Godwin, a sis and
wife of Seth Godwin. Lydia is now dec'd leaving ch: Louisa and
Mary Godwin, minors.

1816
C114-John Hardcastle d 10 Feb 1810, leaving wid, Mary, who m William
Orrell, and ch: Samuel Hardcastle; Ann wife of Thomas Culbreth;
Susan; Philip; John; Robert and William H.C. Hardcastle (last five
are minors).

1818
C122-Isaac Nicols d leaving Edward; William; Tilghman; Rebecca late
wife of John Handy; Mary and Washington Nicols. Rebecca left
three children: Theodore, Louisa and John Handy.

1818
C128-John Carter re: NEIGHBOR'S KINDNESS, WHITE'S DISCOVERY, HONEY-
SUCKLE, TROTTER'S LOTT (one of originals of LLOYD'S REGULATION),
BEACOM'S LOTT.

1816
C134-Levin Noble seized of MT. ANDREW, NABBS CEASANT, DOUBLE PURCHASE
d leaving wid now living and ch: Nancy wife of William Williams;
Tamsey who m Thomas Hurt and d; Charity Noble; Levin Noble; Caleb
Noble; Nathan Noble; Summers Noble; and the petitioner, William
Noble, all of ROSS CO, OHIO. William Noble, an uncle, occupies
the farm.

1819
C141-Matthew Hardcastle re: COLE BANKS ENLARGED.

1819
C147-John Dawson d April or May 1798 in CAR with will. Devised BLACK
LEVEL ENLARGED and ADDTN TO RAWLEIGHT to son, John, and other
lands to other persons. Wid, Sarah, since dec'd, leaving four
sons and two daus. George Dawson d before his bro, John, intestate, leaving Enoch, William, Medford, Sarah, Mary and Asbury,
last three minors. Noah d before his bro, John, leaving Ritta
wife of John Graham; Elizabeth wife of Thomas Anderson; Edward;
Mary; Richard; Zaccheus; John Jefferson, and Sarah, last four
minors. Sarah has since d. Sovren Dawson, a son, is the petitioner. John Dawson, a son, died intestate, without heirs; Mary
Dawson, a dau, wife of James Derickson; Sarah Dawson, a dau, wife
of Cyrus Bell.

1819
C153-William Kelly d 1 January 1815, possessed of OUT RANGE, WADDELL'S
VENTURE; POTTER'S HAZARD or HENRY'S HAZARD. Left ch: Elizabeth
m Jesse Hubbard; Ann who d without issue; Deliza who m Andrew
Barton; William Kelly and Paulson Kelly(last two are infants).

1819
C158-William Bell d 1815 leaving Daniel Bell, Jr; Nancy Bell; Mary
Bell who m Levin Smith; William Bell; Margaret Bell; Robert Bell;
and Henry Bell(last four are minors). He owned MILL SECURITY,
PLOWYARD, FOUNTAIN'S ADDITION to WHITE'S BEGINNING, PINEY NECK
REGULATED, EXCHANGE, LYCONIUM, LECOMPTE'S LOT, CAPE ANN, HALLOCK'S

COW PASTURE, SAND HILL, BYRN'S BOWER, PARROTT'S LOOKOUT.

1821
C166-John Clough and Robert Jarman re: BANK'S ADDITION.
Robert Norvill, 60 years(1820) ment: Solomon Mason, James Williams,
Jadwin Monticue, James Roddis, DICKINSON'S PLAINS, Joseph Boon.
Joel Clements, 38 years(1820) ment: his father, James Clements;
Charles Emory, John Green, William Nailor, MERRICK'S DELIGHT.
John Longfellow, 41 years(1820) ment: his father, Amos Longfellow;
William Starkey; Anthony Chilton; Thomas Hopkins; Robert Orrell.

1822
C170-William Hughlett re: LONG MARSH RIDGE ENLARGED, MARSH LAND, EDEN
KELLY, HOG PEN NECK.

1822
C174-Joannes Gland d 1791 leaving ch: Milley, Elizabeth, Mary, Samuel,
Edward and Violet. Milley d without issue; Mary m John Beacham
and d leaving two ch: William and Edward Beacham. Elizabeth lives
in VA. Samuel d without issue. Edward d without issue. Violet
m James Mungan.

1822
C183-John Irvin d 1800 leaving ch: John, Elizabeth, William, Susan and
Nancy. Elizabeth m Charles Jewell, KENT CO DEL, and d leaving
Henrietta, Margaret and Rachel Jewell, infants. Susan m William
Jewell, son of George Jewell. Nancy d without issue. Irvin owned
PINEY NECK and EXCHANGE.

1822
C196-Thomas W. Dawson, SUSSEX CO DEL, d 24 Dec 1817 leaving wid, Tabby
Dawson, and ch: Sally Thomas Dawson wife of Morgan Williams; _
Elizabeth Wingate Dawson wife of Jesse Wright, about 20 yrs;
Edward Dawson; Cannon Dawson; Mary W. Dawson; Joseph Dawson;
Thomas W. Dawson; William W. Dawson and Margaret Ann Dawson, all
minors. He owned CANAAN IMPROVED, BROWN'S LUCK and WATER'S
FRIENDSHIP.

1821
C207-John Baynard, KENT CO DEL, d owned MT. HOLLY, TURPIN'S DISCOVERY,
CHANCE. Left widow, Margaret, and ch: Elizabeth wife of Henry
Casson; Mary wife of James Baynard; Robert C. Baynard; John Bay-
nard; Sarah Baynard; Margaret Baynard; Thomas Baynard; Ann Baynard;
and Ferdinand Baynard(last four are minors).

1816
C211-William Webb d possessed with LYFORD, leaving ch: Levinah wife of
Thomas Sylvester; James; William; Samuel; Rachel and Washington
Webb(last five minors).

1820
C216-William White d 1 July 1817, owned WHITESBOROUGH DIVIDED leaving
Henry White of PHILA; William, Margaret Ann, Sarah and Elizabeth
White(last four minors).

1821
C222-Levin Baynard d March 1820 leaving Anna wife of John Councill;

John Baynard; Levin Baynard; Nancy wife of Samuel Craddick;
Elizabeth wife of Abner Roe of William. She is now dec'd. John
Baynard has d leaving Levin, John, William, Baynard and Anna Bay-
nard(all infants). Levin Baynard owned RERESBY, GARRETT'S LOOKOUT,
SANDY HILL, MARY'S GARDEN, JACKSON'S MEADOWS, BYRNS BOWERS, GLASCO,
PINEY NECK,REGULATED, MAIDEN'S FOREST.

1822
C240-John Barwick d possessed with PARTNERSHIP. His widow, Deborah,
    m William Colston. His dau, Anna, m John Roe; and his dau, Jane,
    m William Auld. He also left Serena, John, Samuel and William
    Barwick who are infants.

1821
C245-John Corrie d 1808 leaving widow, Rachel and ch: James, Sarah and
    Marcey Corrie(last two are minors).

1824
C250-William Camper d seized of GRIFFITH'S PURCHASE and BROWN'S FIRST
    PURCHASE. The heirs, all of lawful age, are: Elizabeth Camper;
    Sarah James, wid; Mary wife of Jacob Covey; Lovey wife of William
    Sewall; John, Rebecca, and Thomas Camper; Tamsey wife of Elisha
    Corkrin and Henry Camper.

1822
C255-John Bradley d possessed with BRADLEY'S ADDTN, FISHER'S MEADOWS,
    HUNTER"S HAZARD, LAINE'S ADDTN, DAFFINS FARM, NEW NOTTINGHAM,
    NEW BUCKBY, GODFREY'S FOLLY, HICK'S PLAINS, AYLOR'S OUTLET, DAW-
    SON'S NECK. His ch: John Bradley; Rebecca wife of Joshua Boon;
    Sarah Bradley, Caroline Bradley and Stephen Bradley(last two
    under 21 yrs.).

1825
D1 -Jesse Wright d July 1807 leaving ch: Peter Wright; Ann Conwell
    wife of William Conwell; Elisha Wright of DEL; Robert Wright;
    Isaac Wright, Jr.; Jacob Wright of IND; Harriett Thompson wife
    of William Thompson of DOR; and Jesse Wright, a minor, of DEL.

1822
D6 -Mrs.Ann Clark re: road petition.

1822
D10 -Joseph Richard pet re: bounds of SHADWELL and LLOYD'S REGULATION.

1826
D14 - William Coursey d October 1821 leaving ch: Samuel Coursey;
    Jeremiah Coursey; William T. Courcey; Anna Maria Fountain;
    Martha wife of John Thawley. Thomas Fountain is d leaving
    Anna Maria, his widow, and two children, Thomas and Edward
    Fountain, the latter now dec'd.

1827
D25 -John Gill re: KIRKHAM'S DISCOVERY.

1829
D28 -Peter Hardcastle is dec'd leaving wid, Mary, and ch: Samuel;
    Anna Maria who m Samuel Vickers; Elizabeth who m Frederick

Harrison; Sarah Rebecca Hardcastle and Henrietta Hardcastle(last two are infants). Sarah Rebecca m Benjamin S. Elliott.

1827
D35 -Elijah Satterfield d 20 March 1825 leaving James Satterfield; Nancy wife of George Prouse; Polly wife of Thomas Hill; Peter Satterfield; Elijah Satterfield; Elizabeth Satterfield and Margaret Satterfield(last three are infants).

1829
D42 -Levin Wootters and Robert T. Keene re: LLOYD'S REGULATION.

1831
D46 -Philemon Harrington d August 1816 leaving wid, Lydia, and ch: Philemon; Serena wife of Aaron Jackson; William; James; Louisa; and Thomas Harrington, all of full age, and also Elizabeth, Maria and Robert Harrington, who are infants. (Robert now dec'd.)

1826
D51 -Christopher Driver d leaving grand-ch. and heirs at law under the will: Peter Pearson and wife, Caroline; Lenora Boon, together with Ann Boon, an infant; Hester Roe wife of James Roe, an infant; Mary Elizabeth Boon, infant; Kitty Driver Boon, infant; and Juliana Boon, infant; all children of William Boon who m Elizabeth dau of Christopher Driver, who also had Peregrine R. Driver and Mary Driver.

1831
D56 -John Clark d 17 April 1813 leaving heirs at law: Richard Clark; Levin Clark; Mary Clark; Elizabeth Clark and Ann Clark who m John Sharp of CAR, she is now d leaving dau, Christiana Clark, infant.

1832
D60 -John Jump d leaving Mary, his wid, and ch: Margaret Jump who m Richard Chambers; Elizabeth who m Emanuel Swift; Mary; Isaac; Henrietta; Martha; Mahala; and Helena Jump(last six are infants).

1830
D68 -William Black d leaving heirs at law: Sarah who m Thomas Swiggett; Robert; Philip and William Black. Sarah is d leaving ch: Mary Elizabeth and Sarah Swiggett. Philip Black is d without issue. William Black is a minor, and Mary Elizabeth and Sarah are minors and live in OHIO and INDIANA.

1825
D72 -Marcey Fountain d leaving ch: Ann wife of Solomon R. Cahall; Marcey Fountain and Alexander Watson Fountain(last two infants).

1831
D76 -Andrew Baggs d middle Oct 1830 leaving wid, Fanny Baggs, and ch: Louisa wife of William Bonwell of KENT, DEL; Bennett Baggs; William Baggs of KENT, DEL; Charlotte wife of John Boon, Jr.; Anna Maria Baggs, minor; Andrew Baggs, minor; John Baggs, minor; Frederick Baggs, Minor; Mary Elizabeth Baggs, minor(now d a few weeks after her father.)

1831
D84 -Samuel Harrington, KENT, DEL, d Feb 1813 or 1814, leaving wid,
Sarah, and ch: Thomas B.; Henry; William; Samuel; all of full
age and Peter Harrington, a minor, all residing in KENT CO, DEL.

1832
D89 -Batchelder Chance d 23 January 1823 leaving ch: Batchelder G.
Chance and Elizabeth D. Skinner wife of Philemon Skinner, of QA.
She d 6 Oct 1824 leaving Caroline D. Skinner, Batchelder C.
Skinner and Elizabeth D. Skinner, all are minors and reside in QA.

1832
D96 -Cornelius Towers d 1827 leaving ch: John; Henry; Margaret wife of
Caleb Bowdle; Mary wife of John Stevens; Esther wife of Benjamin
Nicols; and Ann Towers. Elizabeth Towers his widow. Esther
Nicols and Ann Towers are infants.

1832
D102-Hezekiah Vinson is d leaving ch: Acquilla; Jeremiah and Noah
Vinson. Acquilla is d leaving wid, Nancy Vinson, and ch:
Elizabeth; Maria; Washington; Zebedial and Pratt T. Vinson.
Jeremiah Vinson is d leaving wid, Elizabeth, and ch: Elizabeth,
Ellen, Toifener, May, James, Josephine and Jeremiah.

1833
D106-Henry Friend d 1831 leaving wid, Delia, now m to Thomas Wright,
and ch: John of age; William H. a minor.

1833
D109-George Paine d 1833 leaving wid, Amelia, of KENT CO, DEL, and ch:
William Paine of KENT CO, DEL; Catherine a minor; James a minor;
and Henrietta a minor.

1830
D112-Thomas Goldsborough d 1827 leaving ch: Thomas; Maria T.; Allen
Moore; and Griffin Washington Goldsborough; and also his wid,
Maria Goldsborough. Allen and Griffin are infants.

1834
D120-Charles Ireland d 1813 leaving: James, John, Henrietta wife of
James Carpenter, ELizabeth wife of John Andrew, Isaac, Samuel,
Tamsey and Nancy Ireland(last two are infants). His wid is
Rhoda Ireland.

1834
D128-John and Joshua Boon re: BOON'S PARK

1834
D130-James M. Boon is dec'd,(son of Joseph Boon) and Joseph Boon is
dec'd,(also a son). Their sis, Rebecca wife of Daniel Orrell,
and another sis, Susan Boon. John Thawley m Matilda, wid of
Joseph Boon, and the mother of Rebecca Orrell and her sis, Susan.

1834
D138-Shadrack Liden d 30 January 1833 leaving Edward W.; Ann Adams
Liden wife of Shadrack Liden; William M. A. Liden; Elizabeth
Emily Liden and Shadrack Liden,(last three are minors).

1834
D146-Richard Cheezum d 1827 leaving wid, Elizabeth, and ch: Andrew;
Richard; James N.; Elizabeth Carroll now d. leaving dau, Caroline Carroll; John B.; William L.; Joseph B.; and Mary E. Cheezum. Elizabeth, wid, d 1831; John B. and William L. also are d
under age 21. Caroline Carroll, Joseph B. Cheezum and Mary E.
Cheezum are minors.

1833
D151-Woolman Hughey d 1803 leaving wid, Mary, and ch: Nancy wife of
Newton Andrew; William Hughey; Sarah wife of John Baker; Eliza-
beth wife of Benjamin Baker; Hester wife of Howard Frampton of
TA. Mary Hughey, wid, is now d and William Hughey is also d
leaving Peter, Woolman, Maria, Mary, Elizabeth and William.
Sarah Baker is d leaving son, John Baker, now about 14 yrs.
Elizabeth Baker is d leaving dau, Kitty Baker, now about 13 yrs.

1835
D159-Isaac Baggs and William Pratt are seized jointly in SQUIRREL
SWAMP. William Pratt d since 1820 leaving wid and several ch:
Thomas; Elizabeth; Mary Ann; Rebecca Ann; William H. and
Christopher Pratt - wid is Mary Pratt. Elizabeth has m John
Cahall. Mary Ann; Rebecca Ann; William H. and Christopher are
infants.
Isaac Baggs d since 1820 leaving wife, Mary, and daus: Elizabeth
wife of Robert Smithers; Ann wife of Edward Harper; Sarah Ann
Roe; Mary Baggs; Louisa wife of William Starkey; Hannah; Martha;
Henrietta and Avarilla Baggs of whom last six are infants.

1836
C162-Anna White, DEL, d 1830 leaving heirs: Mrs. Ann Tilghman wife of
William G. Tilghman, Esq., of TA; Samuel W. Polk of NEW ORLEANS;
Daniel Polk of KY; Elizabeth Clayton wid of James Clayton of DEL;
the ch of Mrs. Margaret N. Polk, a sis of said Anna White, and
Mary Cook, a dau of Mrs. Sarah Cook of DEL, another sis of Anna
White. Daniel and Samuel W. Polk are sons of Margaret Nutter
Polk, a sis of Anna White.

1835
D171-Andrew Beachamp d leaving Kitty wife of James Ireland; Nancy wife
of John Huchinson; Elizabeth; John and Levin Beachamp, last two
are minors.

1836
D174-Joseph P.W. Richardson re: MONTPELIER

1836
D177-Matthew Hardcastle, DOR, d and left wid, Mary, and ch: Matthew
W.; Janette who m Madison K. Jacobs, and Edward Hardcastle a minor.

1836
D183-Sarah L. Tilden is d leaving ch: Elizabeth wife of William Dele-
hay; Josephine A.; Charles N.; Thomas W.; Edwin M. and William P.
Tilden. Josephine is now d. and Mrs. Winefred Townsend wife of
Nehemiah Townsend is entitled to her dower.

1836

D190-Harmon Swiggett d 1832 leaving ch: Peter, James, Joseph, Thomas,
Levisa wife of Isaac Stevens, Nancy wife of Azel Stevens, and
John Swiggett. Eben Stafford d with will naming his mother,
Sarah Stafford; Sarah Jane Wootters dau of Sarah, a sis. Also
ment: Matthew Wootters, Mary Ellen Wooters, John Wright, son of
Caleb, Mary Ellen Wright, Tristrum Wright, Nathaniel Wright and
Ann Elizabeth Wright.

1836

D197-John Wilson d 10 Oct 1828 leaving ch: Sarah Ann wife of Joseph
Pearson; Mary M. Wilson who m Batchelder G. Chance(now d leaving
dau, Elizabeth Chance); Eliza Wilson; Thomas M. Wilson and Rebecca Ann Wilson, the last two minors. Sarah Elizabeth is now d.

1837

D203-Henry Kenton d 25 June 1816 leaving ch: William Kenton; Mary wid
of Luther Mason; Elizabeth wife of Thomas Chambers and Elizabeth
D. Kenton who m Harrison Hardcastle, she is now d leaving son,
Thomas Henry Hardcastle, a minor.

1837

D207-William Blake d leaving ch: John W.; Elizabeth A. Saulsbury;
William Blake and Frances Blake. Part of land was sold to Andrew
Manship who d leaving ch: Elijah, Charles, Nathan, Andrew, Mar-
garet A., James and Rachel Manship, last five are infants.

1838

D210-Philip Porter d 1820 leaving four ch: Sarah wife of Thomas Rouch;
Earle who d without issue; Rosannah who m Joshua R. Barwick, now
d leaving three ch: Alexander, Sarah Matilda and Ann Maria Barwick; Susan wife of Elisha Ringgold of QA.

1838

D215-Levin Wootters re: LLOYD'S REGULATION and NEIGHBORS KEEP OFF.

1835

D228-Nimrod Barwick d leaving ch: White; Matilda wife of Elijah Bartlett; Juliett; Catharine Maria; Mary Ellen; Ann; William Alexander
and Lucy Agnes Barwick, now dec'd. Last five are infants.

1837

D235-William Wilson d 1835 leaving wid, Rebecca, and heirs at law,
William, Robert, Rachel J., Ann and Hester Wilson. Last four
are minors.

1838

D243-Joshua Boon d 10 Aug 1837 leaving John Francis Boon and Charles
Edmond Boon, a minor. Also ment: Rebecca Boon.

1838

D248-William Jones d 21 January 1838 leaving ch: Richard Jones and
Emeline wife of John Downes of QA and Sarah Elizabeth Spencer,
a minor, dau of Jonathan and Catharine Spencer, a dau of William
Jones. The wid, Allanora Jones, now living.

1840
D257-Joseph Vicers, SUSSEX, DEL, d 1837, leaving wid, Mary, and two
     children and three gr-children: Catharine Vickers wife of John
     H. Twiford; Elizabeth Vicers, dec'd's youngest dau; and Joseph
     V. Davis; Mary C. Davis and Amelia V. Davis, ch of Amelia wife
     of James Davis, a dau of dec'd.

1837
D288-Joshua Noble d 1830 leaving wid, Sarah, and ch: Charles Noble;
     Elizabeth wife of Anthony Adams; Solomon Noble; Esther wife of
     Charles Smith; James; Alexander; Amelia; William; Twiford and
     Jane Noble. Last three are infants.

1840
D295-Aaron Clark d 1839 leaving ch: Ann wife of Thomas Wheeler; John;
     William; Caleb; Charles Wesley; Mary Elizabeth and Emeline Clark.
     Last four are minors. His widow, Lydia Clark, is living.

1840
D309-James Holding d 1825 leaving brothers and sisters: Nancy who m
     William Budd; Elizabeth who m Nathan Davis; Sarah who m James
     Geadson, he is d, she then m Benjamin Hargrove; Matilda who m
     Caleb Hargrove; William; and Risdon(called Reuben) Holding. The
     last four named now residents of OHIO. Elizabeth Holding wid of
     dec'd.

1842
D314-Bing Whiteley d leaving wid, Rebecca, and ch: William, Daniel,
     Sarah, Mary Ann and Thomas Bing Whiteley.

1839
D320-Nancy Lyden(formerly Nancy Fountain) d 1833 leaving heirs: Sarah
     Fountain now Sarah Lyden; Keturah Fountain now Peters; Zabdiel
     Fountain, a minor, and Shadrack Lyden. William Lyden and Sarah,
     his wife, presented the pet.

1840
D326- James Dukes d October 1842 leaving ch: Sarah Ann wife of Edward
     Hardcastle; Elizabeth; Levi T.; Rebecca Ellen; James Kent; John
     Boon and Isaac R. Dukes. Last six are minors.

1840
E1   -Anderton Fountain d 1 February 1829 leaving Sarah Fountain wife
     of William Lyden; Kitturah Fountain now Stevens and Zabdiel
     Fountain, a minor. He owned WILLIAMS DELIGHT, GOLDSBOROUGH'S
     REGULATION, MURPHEY'S FORTUNE, HARVEY'S LOT, HACKETT'S ADDTN,
     RICHARD'S ADDTN.

1844
E7   -Anderton O. Breeding d 1837 leaving ch: Elizabeth who m Peter
     Hubbard; Hester Breeding; Mary Stevens Breeding; Matilda Bree-
     ding; Sally Ann Breeding; Ellender Breeding; and Anderton Lewis
     Breeding. Last three are minors. The wid, Ellender, has m
     Daniel Willson. Dec'd owned CHANCE'S DESIRE.

1837
E13 -Richard Skinner d 1837, leaving wid, Sophia E. Skinner, and ch:

Richard A.; Thomas E.; and Sophia King Skinner, a minor. He
owned farm called CONTROVERSEY.

1844
E23 -James Newlee d April 1842 leaving wid, Kezia Newlee, and heirs:
Warner Newlee; Hannah who m James Jarman; Sarah who m William
Scott, KENT CO DEL; Elizabeth; Martha and George. Last three
minors. Newlee owned EWINGTON, KILL MAIDEN'S ADDITION, FORREST
LODGE, WHEELER'S CHANCE and KILL MAIDEN.

1846
E33 -Garretson Turner d October 1845 and left wid, Sarah, and ch:
Zachariah; Maria; Richard; Elizabeth who m Joseph McMahan; Henry;
William; Elizabeth Anne; Mary Jane who m William Mandrell; Mar-
garet Ellen; Sally; Harriet; Nancy Catharine; Edna Francis; and
Martha Turner. Last nine are minors. Turner owned RYE MOLE,
JONES ADDITION TO GOOD HOPE, TAYLOR'S KINDNESS, LAMP HIGH,
NANCY'S DELIGHT, BATTLE HILL and LANE'S VENTURE. Solomon Robin-
son m Sally Turner, the dau. His gr-dau, Mary Eliza d July 1849
intestate. Her father, Henry Turner d leaving wid, Rachel, who
is now m to Elijah Satterfield.

1850
E61 -Nicholas Fountain d 21 November 1843 leaving a wid, Hester A.,
now m to Benjamin Atwell, and ch: Caroline E. m to William S.
Carroll; Mary Ann, now d and John Thomas Fountain, a minor.
Fountain owned CONTROVERSY and LOGAN'S HORNS.

1851
E82- Joseph P.W. Richardson d 1838, left a wid, Lucy B. Richardson,
and ch: Ann Wm. S. who m Charles A. Griffith; Sally L. who m
Edward D. Martin; Elizabeth G.P. who m James B. Steill; Joseph
P.W. Richardson; Rufus K. Richardson and Lucy B. Richardson.
Last three are minor. Richardson owned LYFORD, MONTEPELIER,
DUKE'S ENTERPRISE, SEWELS RANGE, BENNET TOLSON and SCARBOROUGH.

1852
E102-James Carter d 22 May 1849 leaving a wid, Araminta, and ch:
Ellen M. Horsey; William G. Carter; Margaretta Carter and James
Carter. Last three are minors. Samuel H. Horsey m. Ellen M.
Carter.

1853
E110-Elizabeth Skinner d 1832 leaving her husband, Philemon Skinner,
and ch: Bachelder C. and Elizabeth. Bachelder m Emily C. ____
and Elizabeth m John Coursey, both since dec'd leaving James P.
and John William Coursey. Philemon Skinner is dec'd. She owned
BEAR POINT, TAYLORTON, INGRAM'S DESIRE, IRISH DISCOVERY, BAKER'S
PLAINS, CHANCE'S LOT, CONCLUSION, ADDTN TO NOD, BANK'S DELIGHT,
HICKORY RIDGE.

1855
E117-Robert Jarman d 1851 leaving a wid, Sarah, and ch:and gr-ch:
Wesley Jarman; William T. Jarman, Robert N. Jarman, Susan the
wife of Joshua Melvin, Elizabeth wife of Theodore R. Straughn,
Charlotte Jarman, Louisa Jarman. Also Robert and Thomas Henry
Coursey, two ch of Mary Jarman Coursey; William Thomas Jarman son

of James Jarman, a son of dec'd. Sally Ann Duke, wife of John
Duke, a dau of dec'd.

1858
E124-Robert Orrell d 1835 leaving two ch: Henry and Margaret Orrell,
seized of ORRELL'S CHANCE. Margaret m a Derochbroune. Henry is
d leaving one ch, Rober J. Orrell, a minor.

1858
E130-William Dillon d 1824 leaving ch: Ann m William Lucas; William
Dillon; Susan Dillon; John Dillon; Jane E. Dillon who m Zenos
Dawson; Sarah Dillon who m James Kelly; Clementine Dillon who
m Thomas Stevens, both dec'd, leaving dau, Elizabeth Stevens;
James Dillon; Elizabeth Dillon who m Samuel Wright; and Ann M.
Stevens, the ch of Clementine Dillon. Elizabeth Wright now d.
William Dillon owned RETALIATION.

1859
E140-Sally Ann Keene d 1847 possessed of EDEN KELLY or LONG MARSH
RIDGE. She left William M. Warner and Catharine E. Keene,
minors.

1859
E147-Nehemiah Saulsbury d 1836 leaving a son, John R.T. Saulsbury,
and dau, Lusinda Saulsbury. He owned MT. ANDREW , LLOYD'S
REGULATION and SHADWELL. Lusinda m a Foster and d leaving
only ch who has d leaving James R. Saulsbury; Sarah Pearson;
Maria Pearson; Ann Kelly and John R.T. Saulsbury. Maria
Pearson has d leaving William T. and Sarah C. Pearson. Ann
Kelly has d leaving Mary Amanda wife of Richard Bishop.
John R.T. Saulsbury is d leaving Kate Fountain Saulsbury and
Corine Saulsbury.

1859
E159-Thomas Turner d 1846 and left two sons, Samuel and Thomas Turner,
Jr. The latter d March 1849 leaving a wid, Sarah, and ch:
James H., Ozella and Samuel Turner, all minors.

1860
E164-Edward W. Liden d 1852 leaving a wid, Sarah R., and ch: Nancy
R. the wife of Isaac K. Wright; William E.; Sarah A.; and
Elizabeth E. Liden. Last three are minors. Liden owned CABBIN
RIDGE, OUT RANGE, STEVENS BEGINNING, WADDELS VENTURE. Gootee
Stevens m Sarah R.-G. W. Collison m Ann-Sarah A. Liden m Francis
Neal.

1861
E177-John Thawley d last part of 1854, left ch: Louiza wife of Marcy
Fountain; and Matilda Thawley, his wid; Elizabeth wife of Edgar
Plummer; John; George; and Andrew J. Thawley, and Sarah E. dau
of William E. Thawley, a dec'd son; and Bennett, John, Mary Louisa
and William Jones, the ch. of Mary Thawley who m William L. Jones.
Com: William H. Downes, R.E. Hardcastle, Henry Straughn, William
Roe, William B. Massey. John Thawley owned fourteen separate
farms in CAR and QA. Dwelling plantation was WIDOWS CHOICE and
part of COURSEY'S NEGLECT. Other farms were BURNT HOUSE FARM,
tenant, William Turner. BRIDGETOWN FARM, tenant, William Downes.

41

His rights in a farm in Tuckahoe Neck(un-named). CHURCH FIELD farm in QA occupied by George Thawley. ABNERS PARK in CAR adj Edgar Plummer, Thomas Jones and John Clough. Farm where William Thawley lived and died, now occupied by Thomas Pippin in QA. Woodlot in CAR bought of James Anthony. Woodlot in CAR known as SPRING VALLEY. Lots in Bridgetown and on the road to Boonsborough.

1863
E197-Short A. Willis d 3 October 1860 leaving a wid, Mary Willis and ch: Mary E. wife of James M. Jones; Arthur J.; Peter J.; and Richard S. Willis. Peter and Richard are in Texas.
Com: Tilghman Hubbard, Job D.A. Robinson, Barrett Potter, John Nicols, William Sisk. Willis owned RETALIATION, PINEY POINT, and PROVIDENCE.

1860
E204 Amelia Reed d 1859, left no husband, had ch. and gr-ch: W.W. Reed; Jesse W. Reed; Elizabeth W., wid of Daniel Cannon of DEL who are only ch and Margaret, wife of William Robinson; Mary E. Reed; John Reed and Amelia Reed of DOR, ch of son, John Reed, dec'd. Last three are minors.
Com: Daniel Fields, William S. Goslin, Alcaid Dawson, Nathaniel Davis, Levin Stubbs.

1865
E210-John Williams d 20 Dec 1861, left ch: Mary W. wife of Joshua Seward, Jr.; Wilhimenia T.; Luther; Laura V.(since d without issue) and Ella Moore Williams; and his wid, Elizabeth P. Williams. Last three ch are infants.
Com: William R. Massey, William A. Ford, Henry Straughn, William Connelly, William A. Barton. Wilhimenia m Jonathan Evitts.

1864
E222-Amelia Charles d intestate seized of land willed to her by her father, Mark Noble, and left ch: Celia wife of Charles Wright, and Sarah Ellen and Mary Catharine Wright, infant ch of their dec'd mother, Mary Wright, a dau.
Com: Willis Corkran, Henry Mobray, William Stack, Curtis Davis, Alcaid Dawson.

1876
E232-Elizabeth Todd d 10 March 1868 leaving heirs: John W.B. Todd; Elijah Todd; Martha J. who m Alexander W. Lord and Mary E. who m Samuel H. Fluharty, and a gr-dau, Aramintha Wright, child of dec'd dau, Martha Elizabeth Ann Wright.
Com: James E. Douglass, Madison Williams, Dr. Henry F. Willis, Matthew Patton and Tilghman H. Hubbard.
Farm #1 -PAINTERS RANGE, TAYLOR'S RAMBLE and HAZZARD, whereon David Todd d, now occupied by Alexander Lord. Farm #2-HAB NAB AT A VENTURE. David Todd d 1 June 1870, leaving wid, Rebecca Todd, now living. He was gr-fath of Aramintha Wright.

1878
E251-Daniel Sparklin d September 1876, seized of OUT RANGE, WADDELS VENTURE, HARRY'S SETTLEMENT ENLARGED, HARRY'S HAZZARD, leaving ch: Eli; Angelina wife of William H. Mobray; Silas; Martha wife of Francis Collins; Lydia and Walter Sparklin.

1878
E261   Stephen H. Anderson d November 1871, leaving widow, Rachel, and ch:
       Isaac D. who m Roxie A. Spurry; Mary E., who m William J. Wilkinson;
       Emily; Sarah E.; Laura; Annie E.; Lucinda; Clementine; Edward F.;
       William H.; Robert L.; Rachel V. and Roberta M. Anderson. He owned
       the BEGINNING and HILLS OUTLET.

1883
E271 Thomas Everngam d 1880, owned farm DUKEDOM. His son, Joseph Everngam
      is dec'd, leaving no widow, and ch: Mary J.D. wife of Charles H.
      Clark, Thomas H., Charles J., John L., Minnie L., Bertha M. and Emma
      M. Everngam.

1883
E278   James E. Douglass d December 1880, leaving ch: James H., Joseph,
       Thomas H., Samuel E., and Stephen E., also a widow, Mrs. Ann E.
       Douglass.

1884
E298   John E. Starkey d leaving ch: Ellen T. wife of John A. Downes; Charles
       E.; John M.; William C.; Franklin P.; Isabella V. the wife of Thomas
       Cecil and Thomas B. Starkey.

1884
E298   John E. Starkey d January 1, 1883 seized of BRADLEY FARM, 800 a.,
       leaving ch: Ellen T. Downes wife of John Downes; Charles E. Starkey;
       John M. Starkey; Wm. C. Starkey; Franklin P. Starkey; Isabella V.
       Cecil; and Thomas B. Starkey and Marion Starkey.

1895
F1   James P.J. Hubbard, TA Co, d April 1894, seized of JACKSON FARM in TA
      Co and HOMESTEAD FARM, GIFFORD FARM; HOG ISLAND PLACE; TOY LOT; BEULAH
      LOT and BOOBY OWL FARM, all in Caro Co, leaving survivors: Winnie B.
      Hubbard, the wife of Wm. R. Fountain, P. Howard Hubbard and Emma S.
      Hubbard, his ch. and Martha Hubbard his widow. Emma S. is an infant
      and P. Howard is mentally incapacitated.

Brackets [] are used to show additional genealogical information taken from chancery case, not found in the docket.

1. Henry Martindale, Price Martindale, Mary Martindale the elder, Richard Martindale, Mary Noble, otherwise called Mary Martindale and Elizabeth Martindale vs. John Martindale and Jacob Pratt. 1815.
    Thomas Saulsbury, Solomon Brown and Samuel and Jonathan Neal vs. Charles Wright and Maria Wright, heirs of Levin Wright of Levin [d Dec 1812]. 1815.

2. William Whitely, Brown & Culbreth use of Solommon Brown and John W. Bowley admr of John Fisher vs. Samuel Hardcastle, Philip Hardcastle, John Hardcastle, Robert Hardcastle and William H. C. Hardcastle, heirs at law of John Hardcastle, decd. 1815.
    Collins Carey, trustee of Edward E. LeCompte vs. Beachamp Stevens.

3. Anthony Ross vs. Selah Ross, Kitty Ross, Eli Ross, Lovey Ross, heirs at law of Pritchett Ross, decd [d 1814]. 1815.
    William Potter vs. Nicholas Fountain, Walter Lane Fountain, Giles Hicks and Henny his wife, Marcy Fountain and William Fountain, heirs at law of William Fountain, decd [d 15 March 1807] . 1816.

4. Anthony Ross [of TA Co], use of William Hughlett vs. Elizabeth Richardson [age about 11 yrs] , James Richardson [aged about 9 yrs], Sarah Ann Richardson [age about 7 yrs], William Richardson [age about 3 yrs] and Benjamin Richardson [age about 8 mos], children and heirs at law of Thomas Richardson, decd [d 27 Dec 1815]. 1816.
    William Potter vs. Ann Harvey, Levina Harvey, Easter Harvey, John Harvey, Samuel Harvey and Mauliff Harvey, children and heirs at law of John Harvey, decd [d about 1 Jan 1813].

5. William McCollister [age about 19 yrs, son of Feaby McCollister] by Joshua Polk, his next friend and William Haskins and William Meloney, creditors of John McCallister. 1816.
    William Grason vs. Nimrod Barwick and Ann, his wife, Thomas Sylvester and Levinah his wife, James Webb, William Webb, Samuel Webb, Rachel Webb and Washington Webb, heirs at law of William Webb. 1816.

6. Edward Swift use of Thomas Culbreth vs. George Newlee and Mary his wife, of Caroline Co, William Nickerson and Sarah, his wife, Andrew Mundice(?) and Cornelia his wife, Charlotte Burt, Harriott Burt, Joseph Parris and Mahala his wife, non-residents and heirs at law of Eli Burt, decd [d 1806]. 1817.
    Henry Ward by Seth Godwin, his trustee, vs. William Harris and Lucretia his wife, Daniel Ward of James, Mary Wright, William Kelly and Rachel his wife, Daniel Wright of A., Louisa Godwin and Mary Godwin of Caroline County and Peter Wright and Rachel Wright, non-residents. 1817.

7. William Harris, jun., vs. Hannah Kelly, Hicks Kelly, Sylvester Kelly, Martin Kelly and Dennis Kelly, children and heirs at law of Dennis Kelly, decd [d about 15 Jan 1814]. 1817.
    Kimmel Godwin vs. Thomas Garrett, infant child of Thomas Garrett, decd. 1817.

8. Henrietta Byrn vs. Maria Byrn, William Byrn, Ann G. Byrn and Caroline Byrn, children and heirs at law of James Byrn, decd [d 2 Sep 1816]. 1817.

William Talboy guardian of the infant children of Elijah Russell, decd, vs. Elizabeth Edmundson and Edmondson Rogers, heirs at law of Joshua Driver, decd. 1817.

9. Philemon Plummer vs. Thomas Forsythe, Ann Swiggett, Luther Swiggett and Catharine Swiggett, children of Levin Swiggett and Peggy his wife, decd, and infants, Henry Webster, Peggy Webster, Thomas Webster, Richard Webster and Easter Stafford, children of Joseph Stafford and Sarah, his wife [dau of Levin Smith], decd, infants John Smith, Edward Smith of Nathan, an infant; Frances Reynolds, widow [widow of Thomas Reynolds and dau of Levin Smith], Levin Smith and Mary Smith, heirs at law of Levin Smith. 1817.

Samuel Milbourn and Sarah, his wife, vs. James Pippin and Tristram Pippin. 1817.

10. Thomas Saulsbury and Styll and Sylvister vs. Rhoda Wright, widow of Jacob Wright, William Wright and Celia his wife; Ann wife of Daniel Wright, Harris Wright, Lemuel Wright, James Wright, Edward Wright, Sarah Wright, Mary Wright, Rhoda Wright and Lydia Wright, children and heirs at law of Jacob Wright, decd. 1817.

John W. Blake for William Blake and Frances Blake, infants both of Talbot County, children of Wm. Blake, decd [d Feb 1813]. 1817.

11. Henry Driver vs. Alexander Hands and Rachel, his wife; James Sangston and Ann, his wife; John Rogers, Elizabeth Edmondson [m Peter Edmondson] and Edmondson Rogers, heirs at law of Joshua Driver [d Dec 1816 without issue leaving descendants of two sisters, Margaret and Elizabeth, as heirs: Joshua D. Robinson, since died intestate and without issue, and Ann wife of James Sangston child of said Margaret and Maria Edmondson who since m Dr. John Rogers and has died leaving infant Edmondson Rogers, Rachel wife of Alexander Hands and Elizabeth Edmondson yet a minor, the children of first named Elizabeth who m said Peter Edmondson]. 1818.

Benjamin Ford and Sarah his wife and William Downes and Ann his wife. 1818.

12. William Monticue vs. Sarah Martindale and John Martindale. 1818.

Adam Foxwell vs Selah Ross, Keturah Ross, Eli Ross and Lovey Ross, children and heirs at law of Pritchett Ross [d Jan 1814], decd and Anthony Ross. 1818.

13. John Graham use of Jacob Charles and Gore Saulsbury use of Thomas Saulsbury, Robert Stevens and George A. Smith vs. Anna Ritta Graham, Thomas Anderson and Elizabeth his wife, Edward, Mary, John Jefferson, Richard Zaccheus and Sovrin Dawson of Caroline County and Cyrus Bell and Sarah his wife of DOR County and others. 1819.

Thoms(?) Coker vs. Lewis Draper. 1819.

14. Joseph Vickers vs. Jesse Brown and James Banning. 1819.

Samuel Talbott and wife, admrx of Charles Manship vs. John Graham and Henrietta his wife; Thomas Anderson and Elizabeth his wife; Edward Dawson, Mary Dawson, John Dawson, Richard Dawson, heirs at law of Noah Dawson. 1819.

15. John Pool vs. Rhoda Wright, widow of Jacob Wright, William Wright and Celia his wife, Daniel Wright and Ann his wife, Harris Wright, Lemuel

Wright, James Wright, Edward Wright, Sarah Wright, Mary Wright, Rhoda Wright
and Lydia Wright, children and heirs of Jacob Wright. 1819.

John Stevens and Mary Everngam vs. Bromwell Andrew, Jeremiah Nicols and
Ritta his wife, Richard Andrew, John Arnett and Mary his wife, Deborah
Andrew, Daniel B. Andrew, Betsy Andrew, Maria Andrew, Tamsey Andrew, a
child, Matilda Andrew, James R. Andrew, Emeline Andrew, Robert Andrew,
Sylvester Andrew, William Andrew, Uphamy Andrew, Harrison Andrew, Seney
Andrew, Tamsey Andrew, a grandhild; James Gowty, Mary Gowty, Elijah Andrew,
Anzel Stevens and Ann his wife; Sally Andrew; Henry Andrew of Dorchester
County, heirs of James Andrew, decd [d about 27 March 1819, leaving widow
Mary Andrew]. 1819.

16. Kimmel Godwin and George Moffett vs. Bathula Wheatley [widow of Wm.
Wheatley], Caleb Wheatley [over age 21], John White and Elizabeth [over age
21] his wife, William Wheatley [under age 21] and Alexander Wheatley [under
age 21], [heirs of Wm. Wheatley]. 1819.

John Emory vs. Thomas [son of Thomas] Roberts and George Moffett.
1819.

17. Levin Baynard vs. Garrett S. Hardcastle, Thomas J. Hardcastle, Ann
Hardcastle, Henrietta Hardcastle, Sarah Hardcastle, Philip F. Hardcastle and
Elizabeth Hardcastle, children and heirs at law of Philip Hardcastle, decd.
[Philip Hardcastle d Oct 1815 in Kent Co, Del. Garrett was minor at the
time of death of his father but now of full age; the others are minors
(under age of 21)]. 1819.

Levi Dukes guardian of Elizabeth Mitchell, [dau of John Mitchell late
of Chester Co, Pa] and Eliza Ann Blades [dau of Garretson Blades]. [See
Chancery case of 1831] 1819.

18. William Fleharty for use of William A. [Mc]Keene [of DOR Co] vs. Thomas
Hopkins, Philip Hopkins, Nicholas Hopkins and Elizabeth Hopkins, children
and heirs [and all under age of 21] of Nicholas Hopkins [d in Caroline Co].
1820.

James Johnson vs. James Ireland, John Ireland, Ritta Ireland, Elizabeth
Ireland, Isaac Ireland, Samuel Ireland, Tamsey Ireland and Nancy Ireland,
children and heirs at law of Charles Ireland [d Feb 1818]. 1820.

[Wm. Potter vs Samuel Harvey – that one of the children of John Harvey
namely Samuel Harvey, is an idiot and about 17 yrs old and has an aged and
very poor mother, Nancy Harvey.]

19. Thomas Sullivan and Ellen, his wife vs. David Dean of Eljah. 1820.
Thomas Willis [of DOR Co] vs. Sarah Ann Stanford, heirs at law of
Algernon S. Stanford. 1820.

20. John Allen Sangston vs. Nathan Hobbs. 1820.
State of Maryland vs. Samuel Harvey. 1820.

21. Henry Whitely vs. Elijah Barwick, John Brown of Solomon. 1820.
Nathan Levering [Pres. of Powhattan Manufacturing Co., Enoch Levering,
Jesse Levering, Wm. Wilson junr., Baruch Mullikin and Thomas M. Locke of the
city of Baltimore] vs. Thomas Styll. 1820.

22. William Harris, junr. vs. Hannah Kelly, Hicks Kelly, Sylvester Kelly,
Martin Kelly and Dennis Kelly, children and heirs at law of Dennis Kelly.
1821.

23. John Stevens and Mary Everngam vs. Bromwell Andrews and others, heirs of James Andrew, decd (continued). 1821.

24. Richard Jones vs. Thomas Styll and Rachel his wife. 1821.
Richard J. Jones vs. Robert Sylvester and Mary his wife. 1821.

25. Wm. Hignutt vs. Edward Carpenter and Mary his wife, Mary Stevens, James Stevens, Daniel Stevens and Elizabeth Stevens, heirs of James Stevens, decd [d 9 July 1819, leaving Nancy Carpenter who m Edward Carpenter, Mary Stevens about 18 yrs, James Stevens about 14 yrs, Daniel Stevens about 12 yrs and Elizabeth Stevens about 9 yrs]. 1821.

26. Garretson Turner vs. Mary Ann Eliza LeCompte and Sally Caroline Lecompte of Dorchester Co, Wm. Turner of Caroline County, Mary Andrew of Caroline County, Bromwell Andrew of Caroline County, Jeremiah Nicols and Ritta, his wife of Dorchester County, Elijah Andrew of Dorchester County, Richard Andrew of Caroline County, Azel Stevens and Nancy his wife of DOR County; Daniel B., Sally, Betsy, Maria, Tamsey, Matilda, James R., Emeline, Robert, Sylvester, William, Eufama Andrew of Caroline County; James Gouty and Mary Gouty of Caroline County; Henry, Harrison, Seney and James Andrew and Tamsey Andrew, the children of Cain Andrew and Rebecca his wife of Caroline County. 1821.

27. Andrew Manship vs. Ann Talboy, heir of Wm. Talboy [junr. who d about 24 Oct 1820, leaving widow Elizabeth and dau Ann a few mos old]].

28. Fred. Holbrook vs. Anderton Ennalls Breeding; James Hubbard and Charlotte his wife; John Wilson and Sterling his wife; Collins Stevens and Betsey his wife; Noah Harper and Vina his wife; and Nancy, Chaney, Anderton, Maria Peters - children and heirs at law of Chaney Breeding. 1821.

29. State of Maryland by Nathan Kirwin vs. Richard Kirwin. 1821.

30. Wm. Hughlett vs. Samuel Draper [full age], Hixon Blades and Traphena his wife [full age], Rebecca Draper [age about 16] , Lewis Draper the son [about age 13] and Margaret Draper the daughter [about 11], John Draper [about 8] and Mary Draper [about 6], heirs and children of Lewis Draper, decd [d 1820. He was married to Margaret ---]. 1822.

31. Joshua Polk vs. Chas. West. 1822.

32. Anthony Whitely Sr. [guardian of John R. and Jesse K. Wright] vs. John R. Wright and Jesse K. Wright [sons of Daniel Wright]. [The case involved land devised to Daniel Wright by Lemuel Wright. During the course of this case Hatfield Wright was appointed guardian to John R. and Jesse K. Wright.] 1822.

33. Kimmel Godwin vs. James Kirwin. 1822.

34. Samuel Longstreet and Joshua Baily vs. Richard Wright. 1822.

35. Richard Hughlett extr of Dekar Thompson vs. Joseph C. Arthur and Samuel Talbott. 1822.

36. Edward and John Collison vs. David; Minos, Richard, Mahala, Sally, Peter Collison, Margaret Collison and Eli Collison and Edward, Ann, Mary Jane, Susan Sophia Collison, children of Minos Collison. [The last four are minors, under age of 21.] 1822.

37. Charles Nicols, Charlotte Nicols and Joseph W. Patterson [of Balt City] vs. [Mary Seth, widow, Alexander Seth under age of 21, Ann Maria Seth under age of 21 and Mary Ellen Seth under age of 21, children of James G. Seth – all residents of Caroline Co]. 1822.

38. John Matthews and George Reed vs. Seth Godwin. Dec 1822.

39. Ann Smith, Thomas Baker and Eliza his wife vs. Chas. W. Smith. 1823.

40. Anna Statia Rhodes vs. Ignatius Rhodes, Philip Rhodes, Geo. Lamdon (alias Lambdin), Henry Lamdon (alias Lambdin), Ann Maria Lamdon (alias Lambdin), Denny Rhodes, Elizabeth Rhodes, Jeremiah Rhodes, Lewis Slaughter and Wm. Henry Rhodes, heirs at law of Lewis Rhodes. 1823.

41. Thomas Roe and Samuel Fountain vs. Polly Roe, Nancy Roe, [both under age of 21] and heirs at law of Wm. Roe. 1823.

42. Richard D. Cooper vs. James Buckmaster and Comfort his wife, Wm. Tomlinson and Eliza his wife, Henry N. Clement and Sally his wife and Maria Cooper, wife of complainant. 1823.

43. John W. Bordley vs. Nathan Keirn. 1823.

44. James Baynard and John T. Miers vs. Thomas and Robert Henry Postlethwaite. 1823.

45. James Webb alias James D. Webb use of Wm. Potter vs. Robert [T.] Keene and Margaret his wife; Eliza, Kitty, James, Edward, Alexander H., Mary Emma Young, of Caroline County and Wm. S. Young of Philadelphia, children and heirs at law [all under age of 21 except William S.] of John Young, decd. 1823.

46. Wm. Potter vs. James Beacham of Q.A. County, Joseph Price and Mary his wife [dau of James Beacham] of Caroline County, Andrew Beacham of TA. County, Celia, Mahaly, William [under age 21], Edward [under age 21], Rhoda [under age 21] Beacham dau of John Beacham, decd; Curtis [under age 21], John, Rhoda and Jeremiah Beacham [who since has died], children of Jeremiah Beacham, decd [d about Aug 1820]. 1823. [Reference is made to Nancy widow of John Beacham. John, Rhoda and Jeremiah Beacham reside in Caroline Co.]

47. Ann Chilton and Thomas Carter, admrs of Wm. Chilton, decd, vs. Rachel [widow of Nathaniel Talbott]; Joseph C., Samuel, Wesly, Charles Edmund Talbott of Caroline County; Arthur and Wm. Talbott of Kent, children and heirs at law of Nathaniel Talbott, decd [d 10 Dec 1820]. [Arthur and William are residents of Kent Co.] 1823.

48. Richard D. Cooper vs. Susan Deford, widow; Price N. Deford, Sally Ann Deford, Emeline Deford, Mary Deford and Henrietta Deford, heirs at law of

Edward Deford [died March 1823]. 1824. [Susan and Emeline reside in Del., Price N., Mary, and Henrietta reside in QA Co, Sally Ann resides in Caroline Co.]

49. Matthew Driver use of James Sangston vs. Joseph Anthony, Thomas Pearson and Ann his wife, Samuel, John [under age 21], Robert Talboy and Eliza[beth] his wife [under age 21], Mary [under age 21], Robert [under age 21] and Lucretia [under age 21] Anthony, heirs at law of Joseph Anthony, decd [d about March 1822]. 1824.

50. Thomas Blades vs. Eliza Ann, Alexander and Nancy Blades, children and widow of Garretson Blades and Wm. Dillon extr of Garretson Blades. [Case involves grist and saw mills devised by Levin Blades to his son Garretson Blades. Nancy Blades widow, m --- Nicols during the course of this case]. 1824.

51. Thomas Potts vs. Mary Eliza Swiggett. 1824.

52. Andrew Manship and Wm. Hughlett [of DOR co] vs. Robert Talboy, Samuel Fountain and Lucretia his wife, heirs at law of Wm. Talboy, decd. 1824.

53. James Sangston vs. Samuel, Risdon, Sophia, Matthew, Lucretia, Anna, Elizabeth, James, Hester, Mary, Edwin, John and Maria Fountain, heirs at law of Risdon Fountain, decd. 1824.

54. Clotilda, Hester, Mary, Joseph, James Council by their mother and best friend. Thomas Wright 3d, guardian. 1824.

55. Thomas Swiggett and James Keene, guardian and next friend of Mary Eliza Swiggett, Sarah Swiggett, Robert Black and Mary Black. 1824.

56. Anthony Ross use of Wm. Hughlett vs. Eliza, James, Sarah Ann, Wm., Benjamin, children and heirs of Thomas Richardson, decd. 1825.

57. Wm. Grason vs. Nimrod Barwick and Ann his wife [widow of William Webb]; Thomas Sylvester and Levinah his wife [dau of William Webb]; James, William, Samuel, Rachel, and Washington Webb, heirs at law of William Webb, decd.

58. Richard Hughlett vs. Ann, Baynard, John, Levin and William Baynard, children and heirs at law of John Baynard, decd. 1825. [Rachel Baynard's note to R. Hughlett withdrawn.]

59. John Stevens, admr of Wm. Dillon; Nancy Dillon widow of William Dillon; Wm. Lucas and Ann his wife; Thomas Stevens and Clementine his wife; Mary, William, James, Elizabeth, Susan, John, Jane, and Sarah Dillon, by John Stevens their guardian. 1825.

60. Mordecai Oxenham vs. Mary, William Henry, Hester Ann Oxenham, heirs at law and legal representatives of William Oxenham [d 1822, leaving widow now dead]. 1825.

61. Thomas Saulsbury vs. James Stack and Eliza his wife, Caleb, Mary Eaton heirs at law of Levi Eaton. 1825.

62. President and Director of Farmers Bank of Md. vs. Eliza, Andrew, George
W. Collison and Nancy Dawson, Elisha Draper and Ann his wife; Matthias Davis
and Priscilla his wife, [heirs of Fountain Collison who d Oct 1824].
[Elizabeth C. widow of Fountain Collison, m Bayard Davis.] 1825

63. Charles and Charlotte Nicols and Joseph W. Pattison vs. Mary Seth,
widow, Alexander Seth, Ann Maria and Mary Ellen Seth, children and heirs at
law of James Seth, decd. 1825.

64. Susan Swiggett for herself and Eliza Ann Swiggett by Susan Swiggett her
sister and next friend vs. Joseph Swiggett and Rebecca Stevens his wife,
William, Gootee, Sarah, Letty, Eleanor, Seney B. Stevens and James Baynard
Stevens, children and heirs at law of William Stevens, decd. 1825.
[See Chancery case: Wm. Potter vs Joseph Swiggett and Rebecca dau of Wm.
Stevens; Sarah Stevens; Vility Stevens; William Stevens; Gowty Stevens;
Ellhanon (son) Stevens; Seney B. (son) Stevens and James A. Bayard Stevens,
children of Wm. Stevens who d Jul 1824. Widow was Vility Stevens.]

65. John Brown vs. Henrietta Brown, Joseph Brown, Wm. Jones and Maria his
wife. 1825.

66. Robert Ewing vs. Mary Wilson, widow; Jonathan, Lewis, Daniel, Job,
Elkany, Balseray, Rachel Wilson, heirs at law of Daniel Wilson. 1825.

69. William Potter vs. Mary Driver, John Brown of Solomon; Joseph P. W.
Richardson admr of Wm. McDonald and James Sangston. 1826.

71. James Dukes, guardian to Deborah, Margaret, Thomas, and Charles
Saulsbury, infants [and children of Chas. Saulsbury]. 1826.

72. Thomas S. Carter vs. Alford, Mary and Hester Ann Driver, minors and
children and heirs at law of Matthew Driver, decd. 1827.

74. William Potter vs. William A. Ford of Caroline County, Thomas H. Ford,
Samuel Satterfield and Maria his wife of TA. County, Belliza Ford, Caroline
and Marietta Ford of Caroline County, children and heirs of Thomas Ford,
decd. 1827.

75. James Sangston [resident of Del.] vs. Mary Driver, widow; Matthew, John,
Henry, Joshua, James, Lucian, Theodore Denny, and Eliza Ann Driver, children
and heirs at law of Henry Driver, decd [d 1821]. 1827.
     [James Sangston, Wm. Potter and Kimmel Godwin vs. Alford Driver, Mary
Driver and Hester Ann Driver, children of Matthew Driver of TA Co.]

77. John Brown vs Alice Ann, Susan F., James Hackett [all under age 21],
children and heirs at law of James Hackett, decd. [James Hackett died
leaving 4 children, 3 named above and Jane who is now dead.]. 1827

78. William McKeene [vs Thomas Hopkins, Philip Hopkins, Nicholas Hopkins and
Elizabeth Hopkins, children of Nicholas Hopkins]. 1827.

79. Robert Medford vs. Elijah Jester, Arthur Connelly and Wm. Corkrin.
1827.

80. William Hughlett vs. Mary Meeds, Edwin Meeds of City of Baltimore., John Davis Meeds of Queen Anne's County, infant children and heirs of Malachi Meeds. 1827.

81. James Sangston survivor of Sangston and Whiteley vs. James Plummer, Thomas Atkinson and Mary his wife. 1827.

82. President and Director of Farmers Bank of Md. vs. Barkley Haskins of age, Eliza C. Haskins, minor (Joseph Haskins Bowie, Louiza Emaly Bowie, Isabella Dallas Bowie, Josephine Haskins Bowie, minors), heirs at law of Joseph Haskins [of TA Co]. 1827

83. Kimmel Godwin vs. Arthur Connelly. 1828.

84. Eliza Ross guardian and next friend of Joseph R., Lewis P., Robert W., Charles H., Ann S. and Eliza C. Ross, children and heirs of Anthony Ross, [of TA Co]. 1828.

85. Ann Stockett admr of John Schaff Stockett and Giles Hicks vs. Daniel Dukes and Anna his wife, Marcey Fountain and Sarah his wife, James P., Philemon H., Luther, Edgar, William, Mary Plummer, children and heirs of Philemon Plummer, decd. 1828. Last four children are minors. 1829 - Luther, Edgar, William and Mary are infants; 1831 - William and Mary are infants. [Reference is made to Mary, widow of Philemon Plummer]. 1828.

86. Thomas B. Turpin and James Roe, extrs of James Baynard and John T. Miers vs. Thomas and Robert H. Postlewhaite, children of Thomas Postlewhaite. 1828.

87. Nathan Todd vs. Jesse Hubbard. 1828.

88. James Sangston vs. Charles Leary [DOR Co], Samuel Hardcastle, extrs of Charles Leary, decd, and Sarah Hardcastle, his wife, Elizabeth Rossell [DOR Co], Charles Leary Jr. and Wharton Leary [sons of John Leary who was son of Philemon], heirs at law of Philemon Leary, [who resided in Phila] decd. Bill issued to Somerset County for Charles Leary and Elizabeth Rossell. 1828.

89. Philip S. Derochbrune vs. William B. Tillotson surviving admr of Jacob Dyatt and Alexander Dyatt [under age 21 and residing out of the state], the son and heir of Jacob Dyatt. [The widow and 2 children are decd.] 1829.

90. Richard Chambers and wife, Emanuel Swift and wife, Mary Jump and others vs. James W. Price. 1829.

91. Edmond Owen and Margaret his wife [of Ohio] for use of Archibald Cahall, [of Del.] vs. John Rathell and wife Jane; Solomon R. Cahall and wife Ann, Mary and Alexander Fountain, heirs of Marcey Fountain, Sarah Fountain his widow, James Richardson admr of Marcey Fountain, Jesse Turner, Hester Pratt Turner and Geo. Edward Fountain. [Reference is made to will of 1810 of William S. Turner in which he devised: to mother Milcah Turner, brother Jesse, sister Jane Manlove, sister Margaret Turner, niece Hester Pratt Turner and nephew George Edward Fountain.] 1829.

CHANCERY DOCKET of CAROLINE COUNTY [with annotations]

92. Jeremiah Mullikin and Mary E. [formerly Mary E. Cooke], wife vs.
Clement Fowler. 1829.

93. Jacob Charles vs. Thomas B. Bullock [now decd] and Elizabeth his wife
[dau of Samuel Emerson], Thomas Foster Willis heir of Sarah Willis [dau of
Samuel Emerson], Samuel, Robert and Henry Emerson, heirs of Samuel Emerson,
decd [d 15 Jan 1827]. [Samuel, Robert and Henry are under age of 21] 1829.

94. Lucretia Fountain and George T. Millington, admrs of Samuel Fountain,
decd, vs. James C. Millington and Elizabeth his wife and Elizabeth Ann
Talboy, heirs of Robert Talboy, decd [d 20 July 1826, leaving widow
Elizabeth Talboy who married J. C. Millington, and a daughter under age of
21. In 21 Sep 1824 came Samuel Fountain admr of William Talboy, jr, late of
Caroline Co, decd]. 1829.

95. William Hughlett [of TA Co] vs. Joseph Wood and wife Ann, formerly Ann
Chilcutt and Joshua Chilcutt, minor, son and heir of John Chilcutt, decd [d
about 20 Sep 1823]. 1829.

96. Lucretia Fountain and George T. Millington admrs of Samuel Fountain,
decd, vs. Risdon Fountain. 1830.

97. James Sangston vs. Thomas Saulsbury. 1830.

98. George and William Reed vs. Abraham Jump of William, admr of Andrew S.
Green and Andrew Sylvester Green, Henry Valentine Green, and Rachel Jane
Green, minor children of Andrew S. Green, decd [d about 1 Nov 1828 leaving
widow Rachel]. 1830.

99. Jacob Charles admr of Brannock Smith vs. Algernon, William, Mary Maria,
Ann and Deveraux Smith, children and heirs of William (called William G.)
Smith. 1830.

100. Thomas Burchinal, John K. Harper, Jeremiah Burchinal, William
Hughlett, Jonathan Crane, Sarah Milbourne vs. Henrietta Pippin [sister of
James Pippin], William Glanding and wife Ann, Sarah Seward and Rebecca
Seward, heirs of James Pippin of Joseph. [Ann, Sarah and Rebecca are daus
of George Seward, late of QA Co and neices of James Pippin. James Pippin of
Joseph d Sep 1828.] 1830.

101. Bennett Baggs vs. William Baggs. 1830.

102. Thomas Stevens vs. John Stevens and Mark Noble. 1831.

103. Thomas Stevens vs. John Stevens. 1831.

104. Henrietta Brown vs. William Jones and wife Mariah, Norvill T.Brown,
Parthinia Eliza Brown, John T. Brown, Charles C. Brown and Joseph Brown,
children of Solomon Brown, decd. 1831.

105. Isaac Purnell Pendleton, Serena C. Pendleton, infants, by John Boon,
their guardian, vs. Thomas Burchinall admr of Frederick Purnell, Isaac
Purnell and Martha Elizabeth Purnell infants of Queen Anne's County, heirs
of Frederick Purnall [who d 24 Oct 1829 intestate leaving widow Elizabeth
Cook Purnell who resides in Queen Anne's Co, and 2 children, Isaac and

Elizabeth Purnell who reside in Queen Anne's Co. Frederick Purnell was
appointed guardian of the petitioners.] 1831.

106. Pere. Wilmer vs. James McGuire and wife Charlotte. 1831.

107. Short A. Willis vs. Mary Griffith and Levi Griffith. [Levi Griffith d
about 28 Sep 1829, leaving widow Mary Griffith and son Levi his only child,
under age of 21.] 1831.

108. James Dukes vs. Ann widow of Andrew Manship, Elijah, Charles, Joshua,
Nathan, Margaret Ann, James, Andrew and Elizabeth Manship, heirs of Andrew
Manship and Nehemmiah Fountain admr of Andrew Manship. [Under age of 21
are: Charles, Joshua, Nathan, Margaret Ann, James, Andrew and Elizabeth.]
1831.

109. William Hughlett vs. Joshua Chilcutt. 1831.

110. James Sangston and Thomas H. Baynard for use of James Hignutt vs.
Caleb Connelly and wife Ann, Merriam A. B. Oldfield, John Oldfield and
William Oldfield, heirs of Elijah G. Oldfield. 1831.

111. John Boon, admr of Seth Godwin vs. George F. Mason. 1831.

112. Aaron B. Reiner and wife Hester, George Edward Fountain for use of
Joshua Bell, for use of George Fisher vs. John Rathell and wife Jane,
Solomon R. Cahall and wife Ann, George C. Herrin and wife Mary and Alexander
Fountain. 1831.

113. John Allen Sangston vs. Harrison and Thomas H. Hardcastle, Thomas
Chambers and wife Elizabeth. 1831.

114. William B. Tillotson, father, vs. John Tillotson. 1831.

115. Tristram Baggs vs. Sally Ann, Robert S., Ann and Margaret, children of
Elizabeth Baggs. 1832.

116. William Turner vs. Henrietta Brown, widow, William Jones and wife
Maria, Henry G. King and wife Nanette, Eliza P. Brown, John T. Brown,
Charles C. Brown, Levin Charles and Joseph Brown. 1832.

117. Elijah Hignutt and wife Nancy vs. Solomon Dean. 1832.

118. President and Director of Farmers Bank of Md. vs. Nehemiah Robertson
and John R. Roe. 1832.

120. Hannah J. Hackett, mother, vs. Alice Ann, Susan S., and James Hackett
[children of James Hackett, decd]. 1832.

121. William Jones and wife Maria vs. Mary Ann, Wm. T., John Hardesty
[children of John Hardesty], Hutchins H. Smith admr of John Hardesty, decd.
1833.

122. Elisha Willson vs. Jacob Leverton and wife Hannah C., Thomas Sylvester
and wife Euphany, Jacob C. Willson, Elijah Willson, and Martha E. Willson,

children of James Willson, decd [died shortly after signing his will dated 25 March 1824]. 1833.

123. William Jones for use of William Hughlett vs. Nancy, Louiza, Alexander and Rachel Cahall, minors and children of James Cahall, decd [d about 20 Jan 1832] and Archibald Cahall his admr. [Nancy, Louiza and Alexander reside in Caroline Co and Rachel Cahall and Archibald Cahall reside in Kent Co, Del.] 1833.

124. William Glanding and wife Ann, use of Pere Wilmer, use of John Boon, vs. Phenix Virden and wife Ann, Acquilla Starr and Solomon Sparks. 1833.

125. Thomas Richardson vs. Wm. Stevens and wife Ann, William Ross, Henry Cook and wife Lydia; Hester, Mary and Noah Ross, children of Archibald Ross and Peter Barton admrs. 1833.

126. Silas Dunlap vs. John E. Thompson and wife Rutha; James Britton, Ann E. Britton, heirs of James Britton, decd. 1833.

127. John Jump of E[lijah] vs. Peter Jump and wife Ann. [Reference is made to Peter Jump's brother, Zachariah Jump.] 1833.

128. [Wm. H. Crawford, exr of] Samuel Crawford vs. Gore Cahall admr of John Cahall, decd., William B., Solomon, Priscilla, Elizabeth Cahall, children of John Cahall, decd. 1834.

129. William Francis Chilton, James Chilton by themselves, Robert P. and Matthew Chilton by Ann Chilton, their next friend, vs. Matthew Driver, John R. Driver, Samuel Harper and Elizabeth Ann his wife, Henry, Lukean, James and Theodore Driver, infants. 1834.

130. Silas Dunlap vs. Emory Thompson and wife. 1834.

133. Jonathan Spencer vs. Sarah C. Hardcastle, heir of Samuel B. Hardcastle. [Reference is made to Edward Coppage, guardian to Sarah H. Hardcastle] 1834.

134. Henry Rouset vs. Sarah Elizabeth Jones, infant and heir of Curtis M. Jones and Mark W. Foreman, his admr. 1834.

135. Mitchell Covey and Jacob Covey junr. vs. David Dean of Wm. 1834.

136. Elizabeth Ann Talboy and Robert Bishop, her next friend vs. James C. Millington. 1835.

137. Lodman Shields vs. James, Jesse D., Elizabeth and Harriet Ann Hicks; John Eaton Sr., Henry Eaton, Thomas Eaton, John Eaton, Jr., Elizabeth Eaton, Mary Eaton, James Eaton and Levin Eaton, children of John and Rebecca Eaton, decd. [L. Shields d 1836 - Easton Gazette.] 1835.

138. Thomas Burchenal vs. Thomas H. Slaughter, son and heir of Samuel Slaughter. 1835.

139. Abraham Jump for use of Thomas Melvin admr of Hutchens H. Smith vs. Joshua C. Bell [son of Daniel Bell, Senr]. 1835.

CHANCERY DOCKET of CAROLINE COUNTY [with annotations]

140. Thomas Culbreath, John Boon, William Jones, Levin Charles and James Sangston vs Henry G. King and Nanette his wife, formerly N. Brown, Eliza P. Brown, John T. Brown and Charles C. Brown, children of John Brown, decd and Levin Charles, admr of John Brown and John G. Willis. 1835.

141. Marcellus Keene and Mary S., his wife, vs John A. Sangston. 1835.

142. Sarah Jane Jump admr D.B.N. of Samuel Talbott vs. William Arringdale admr of James Ridgaway. 1835.

143. James Sangston vs. Thomas F. Bourke. 1836.

144. Henry R. Pratt the father and next friend of Charles and Thomas Pratt. 1836.

145. George Laws [of Phila, Pa] vs. Mary [widow of Elisha Dawson], Daniel, William, James and Deborah Dawson, wife of Isaac Frampton [heirs of Elisha Dawson who resided outside the state of Md.]. 1837.

146. James Greenlee, hatter, vs. Nehemiah, Thomas H., Hutchens [H.], John W., Eliza A. Smith, heirs of Hutchins H. Smith. 1837.

147. William Hemsley vs. William Turner. 1838.

148. William Turner vs. Thomas Richardson extr of Reuben Richardson, Thomas, Joseph, Ann alias Nancy Richardson, heirs of Reuben Richardson. 1838.

149. William Burt vs. [James M. Downes, husband of] Ann [W.], widow of Asa Burt; Thos. Burt [under age of 22] heir of Asa Burt; George Newlee admr of Asa Burt. 1838.

150. Pere Clarkson free negro vs. Robert Hignutt and Job W. Willson. 1838.

151. Francis Hickman of Pennsylvania vs. Rhoda Rhodes, [widow and] admr of William H[enry] Rhodes, Robert Henry Rhodes [under age of 21], Ann Maria Rhodes [under age of 21] [heirs of William Henry Rhodes]. 1839.

152. James Dukes [who m Ann M. Rhodes dau of Jeremiah Rhodes] vs. William Tolson and others. 1839.

153. Edward B. Hardcastle admr of Thomas Richardson vs. William Stevens and Ann his wife; William Ross; Henry Cook and Lydia his wife; Hester, Mary and Noa Ross, children and heirs of Archibald Ross; and Peter Barton, his admr. 1840.

154. William Potter vs. James Hignutt. 1841.

155. Philemon Skinner vs. Alexander P. Barwick, Matilda Barwick, Ann M. Barwick, heirs of Thomas Burchenal admr of Joshua R. Barwick. 1841.

156. George Cummins and Samuel Catts [of Smyrna, Del.], assignees of Timothy C. Raymond [of Del.] admr of Mary Hardcastle [QA Co, decd] vs. William H. Foster and [wife] Ann R. Foster [widow and] admr D.B.N. of Samuel

Hardcastle [of QA Co] and Sarah C. Hardcastle, heirs of Samuel [B.] Hardcastle. 1842.

157. William B.Smyth vs. Arthur John Willis. 1842.

158. George F. Mason vs. Pere Wilmer, Richard B. Carmichael and Tilghman Johnson. 1842.

159. Zenas Dawson and Jane his wife, formerly Jane Dillon for use of John Pool vs. Levin L. Seward and Nancy his wife formerly Nancy Dillon, widow William Dillon; James Kelley and Sally his wife; James Dillon; Susan Dillon; John Dillon; William Malster; John R. T. Saulsbury; Levi Dukes and Mary Dukes, formerly Mary Dillon, widow of Isaac Dukes; Samuel Wright and Elizabeth his wife, heirs of William Dillon, decd. 1843.

160. Hooper B. Stevens guardian to George Garey and Hooper B. Stevens and John Stack in their own right vs. Zabadiel W. Potter and John L. McCombs. 1843.

161. Levin Wootters vs. Job W. Willson and James Richardson. 1843.

162. Thomas Melvin vs Michael Pinkine. 1844.

163. Sarah Councill vs. George R., Robert, John Smith. 1844.

164. John R. T. Saulsbury and John B. Cooper vs. John B. Thomas use of William H. Henry and John Jump of P., sheriff of Caroline co. 1844.

165. Marcey Fountain admr of Luther T. Plummer vs. Ann Deroachbrune admr of Almira Deroachbrune, Ann C., Philip, Ellen G. Deroachbrune. 1844.

166. George F. Mason vs. Thomas A. Turner and James E. D. Turner extrs of William Turner and John Jump, sheriff. 1845.

167. John Collins vs. Josiah Collins and Thomas Collins of J. 1846.

168. Zebediah Turner vs. Maria, Richard and Elizabeth Ann Turner. 1846.

169. James Stack vs. William A. Barton, Thomas F. Garey and Elizabeth Stack. 1846.

170. Frances E. and Arthur Foreman vs. Marcellus Plummer and others. 1847.

171. Job W. Willson vs. Charles Peters, James Hignutt and William Delehay. 1847.

172. Ennalls Hubbard vs. Robert Smith and Rachel, his wife and Elenah Willson. [Balscray Willson and Elkany Willson held undivided moiety of tracts, Hampstead and Kirkham's Discovery. Balseray d 1847, leaving heirs: his brothers and sisters, namely Jonathan Willson, Daniel Willson, Job Willson, Rachael Smith wife of Robert Smith, and Elkany Willson]. 1847.

174. Israel Griffith vs. James R. Hopewell and Maria Antoinette his wife, Philip Culbreath, Thomas E. Culbreth. [Israel Griffith of Balt City is a creditor of Thomas Culbreth of Caroline Co, who d 1843 intestate, leaving

Maria Antoinette wife of James R. Hopewell of St. Mary's Co, Md.; Philip Culbreth of Caroline Co and Thomas F. Culbreth of Balt City, as his heirs – as also Mary Reed Culbreth a minor his heir who is since decd intestate and without issue. Thomas E. Culbreth is under age of 21.] 1851.

175. John G. Miller and Sarah H. his wife [of New York City] vs. Frederick M. Fountain [of said city], infant. [William Thomas Fountain d 1843 leaving widow Sarah H., and two children, Thomas C. and Frederick M. – Shortly thereafter Thomas C. died.] 1851.

176. Jacob Morgan and Henrietta his wife formerly Henrietta Thawly vs. Henrietta Thawley, widow of William decd, Mary E. Thawley, Caroline Barton, widow of James H. decd, William Willson, Thomas C. Willson, Robert E. Willson, Robert E., Mary H., Jacob F., Philip A., Anna L. and Caroline Morgan, children and heirs of William Thawley, decd. [William Thawley, late of Caroline Co, died in 1850, seized of real estate in Caroline Co, leaving widow Henrietta, now Henrietta Morgan, Mary E. Thawley, Caroline Barton widow of James H. Barton decd (his surviving children) and William Wilson, Thomas C. Wilson and Robert E. Wilson (sons of Sarah Wilson formerly Sarah Thawley a decd dau of Wm. Thawley decd and Robert E. Morgan, Mary H. Morgan, Jacob F. Morgan, Philip A. Morgan, Anna L. Morgan, Caroline Morgan (children of Ann Morgan, decd, formerly Ann Thawley dau of Wm. Thawley). Children of Ann Morgan all under age of 21.] 1851.

177. James Nicols, lunatic, as certified. 1849.

178. William Turner and Margaret A. Turner vs. William H. Rich, Mary F., his wife, Casper M. Newham [Newman of QA Co] and Rebecca his wife, Samuel Betts [of Smyrna Del.] and Harriet E. Betts [of Baltimore City], Charles E. Smith and Elizabeth A. Smith [of Kent Co]. 1851.

179. [Same as above] vs. Samuel Betts, Harriet E. Betts, Charles C. Smith and Elizabeth A. Smith. 1851.

180. William Medford vs. Margaret Medford. [William Medford who m Margaret E. Berry, accuses her of adultery.] 1851.

181. Job D. A. Robinson vs. Purnell Todd and Thomas H. Stack. 1852.

182. Charles B. Jones and Anna Maria Jones by themselves and Sally B. Jones, William Wallace Jones, Joseph B. Jones and Benjamin F. Jones by guardian, Charles B. Jones vs. Henrietta Jones and James D. Jones. [William Jones died intestate Nov 1848, seized of a tract of 400 a. where he resided at his death and also a lot in Denton on S.E. corner at 2nd and Gay streets; also lot on 2d street which is subject to life estate of Mrs. Solomon Brown of Mississippi. 1852.

183. Bayard Davis and Matilda Davis his wife vs. Araminta Carter. 1852.

184. George Fisher vs. John L. McCombs and James H. Barwick. 1852.

185. Thomas Smith vs. Robert S. Bryan. 1852.

187. Sorden Kinnamon and Ann Maria, his wife; Mary Ellen Kinnamon; Hugh B. Simpers and Elizabeth his wife vs. Nathan Ginn. 1853.

188. Richard Jester and Dorcas his wife vs. Solomon Truitt. 1853.

189. William Sapp vs. Robert H. Rouse. 1853.

190. James H. Holmes and Barrett Patton vs. Peter Todd, Edward Hardcastle, John W. Hignutt. 1854.

191. Charles Lain vs. Robert Jarrell extr of Richard Jarrell, decd. 1854.

192. Thomas Jones vs. Susan Jones. 1855.

193. Amelia Reed formerly dau of Isaac Wright [late of DOR Co who d about 23 Jan 1850]] vs. Curtis Davis, Sylvester H. Smith; William H. Watkins and William Stack. 1855.

194. John R. T. Saulsbury and William Loockerman admrs of John C. Cooper vs. John B. Thomas use of William K. Emory. 1856.

195. Levin Dukes and wife Susan vs. William G. Horsey; John Henry Horsey and Elisabeth Ann Horsey. 1856.

196. Thomas and William Loockerman vs. Thomas J. Moore and Francis A. Sisk. 1856.

197. William A. Ford, Clinton Cook and Marietta his wife vs. Caroline Ford. 1857.

198. George E. Sangston vs. James and Mary E. Gooding. 1857.

199. Elizabeth Ann Whitely, minor, by guardian, Thomas F. Garey vs. Valentin Carter. 1857.

200. James H. Barwick vs. John Potts and wife Mary Amanda Potts. 1857.

201. William M. Warner [of Kent Co, Del., son of John Warner late of Caroline Co, decd] vs. Catherine E. Keene; Parrott Roe and Elizabeth Roe. 1858.

202. John W. Temple and Robert Jarrell, admrs of William Temple vs. Samuel C. Young and wife Mariann. 1858.

203. Thomas Andrew of T. Newton Andrew; David Reed and Anna Maria, his wife; William H. Hughey; Thomas A. Hughey; Thomas Stanton and Elizabeth his wife; William Todd and Eleanor his wife; Rebecca Loockerman and Eleanor Hughey vs. William Andrew and Mary his wife and Elizabeth Andrew. [Thomas Andrew of Caroline Co, died 27 April 1853, seized of estate in the Lower District of Caroline Co, leaving Deliah Andrew his dau of Caroline Co who married William Hughey of Del. and has since died as also her said husband, leaving children: Wm. H. Hughey, Ann Maria Hughey who m David Redd, Elizabeth Hughey who m Thomas Stanton of Caroline Co, Thomas A. Hughey and Eleanor Hughey; Eleanor Andrew, a dau who married William Todd of Illinois, Rebecca Andrew, a dau who m Richard Loockerman of Caroline Co which said Loockerman is since decd; Mary Andrew who m Thomas Sullivan of Caroline Co which Sullivan is since decd and said Mary has since m William Andrew; and Elizabeth Andrew of Caroline Co of full age.] 1858.

204.   Ezra M. Hitch and Mary E. Hitch his wife, formerly Mary Wheeler vs.
Lydia A.; Thomas E.; Caleb and Rebecca E. Wheeler. 1858.

205.   John Smith vs. Solomon R. Cahall; Edgar Plummer and Marcy Fountain.
1858.

206.   Thomas J. Moore vs. Thomas Loockerman. 1858.

207.   Sarah Hobbs vs. Titus J. Hobbs. 1858.
       Henry Rousett vs. R. J. Draper. 1858.

208.   Ennalls Hubbard vs. James P. J. Hubbard. 1858.
       James Pool vs. James Stafford and Francis A. Sisk. 1858.

209.   Daniel Orrell vs. Edgar Plummer and George. W. Thawley admrs of John
Thawley. [That Daniel Orrell is entitled to life estate in real estate in
Caroline Co of which Rebecca A. Orrell decd wife of said Daniel Orrell
possessed. Daniel and his children (by said Rebecca) reside on said real
estate. 1858.

210.   Joshua McGonigal vs. William Turner, Alexdr. Knotts and Joseph H. Tarr.
1858.

211.   Thomas F. Garey vs. William Morgan. 1858.

212.   William Boyce vs. Wesley Stack and Alexdr. Knotts. 1858.

213.   John H. Emerson vs. Thomas R.; Maria; Richard and Anna Stewart. [That
around 4 Aug 1848 John H. Emerson sold to Thomas R. Stewart of Caroline Co
(now residing temporarily in the city of Balt) a tract in Caroline Co and
conveyed the same (at the request of said Stewart) to Anna Maria Stewart wife
of Thomas R. Stewart. Anna Maria has since d intestate, leaving 3 children:
Maria, Anna and Richard, all minors.] 1859.

214.   Samuel Thawley use of William E. Chance, use of William E. Mason admr
of Andrew Mason vs. Samuel Dunning extr of B. G. Chance, Ann Maria Smith,
Aaron Smith and Adaline Stanton. 1859.

215.   Theo N. Handy, John Handy and Louisa Russell vs. John Nicols, Susan
Blades, Mary Saulsbury, widow of Thomas; Isaac Nicols; Washington A. Nicols;
Jane Nicols; Margaret Nicols and Charlotte Nicols. 1859.

216.   Charles Lane, guardian to Sarah C. Lane, John F. Lane, Rachel E. Lane,
William B. Golt and John E. Golt vs. George H. Moore extr of Samuel Golt,
John Golt and Sarah Golt, widow. [Samuel Golt of Caroline Co d Sep 1856,
leaving a will in which is mentioned son John and 5 grand children: Sarah C.
Lane, John F. Lane, Richard E. Lane, William B. Golt and John E. Golt. Sarah
Golt, wife of decd Samuel Golt, in 1857 filed in Orphans Court her
renoucement of will.] 1859.

217.   Isaiah C. Blades vs. Ennalls Hubbard and wife Ellen T. 1859.

218.   Ennalls Hubbard vs. James T. J. Hubbard, Josiah Dawson and R. J.
Willoughby. 1859.

219. Ennalls Hubbard vs. Farmers & Merchants Bank of Greensborough. 1859.

220. Warner R. Busteed vs. William Connelly admr of John H. Connelly and Alexdr. Knotts. 1859.

221. George Fisher vs. John W. and Sarah A. Ringold. [That George Fisher of Caroline Co is seized of one undivided moiety of tract called Loggins Horns and Cary's Discovery and the other undivided moiety is held by Sarah Ann Ringgold, wife of John W. Ringgold, it being the cleared land deeded to John C. Cooper and Sarah Ann Cooper by Thomas R. Stewart and wife, 124 a.] 1859.

222. Joel Atwell vs. Elizabeth A. Atwell. 1859.

223. William A. Ford and Joseph K. Cook vs. (no name). 1859.

224. Langstreth and Bailey vs. Richard Wright. 1860.

225. Henry, John, Thomas and Philip Potts, infants and heirs of Thomas Potts, decd, by Joseph Boon, guardian, vs. Mary E. Swiggitt. 1860.

226. Thomas Saulsbury vs. James Stack and wife Elizabeth; Caleb and Mary Eaton, children and heirs of Levin Eaton. 1860

227. James Sangston sur. of Sangston & Whiteley vs. James Plummer, Thomas Atkinson and wife Mary and Silas Hicks. 1860.

228. Thomas Stevens vs. John Stevens. 1860.

229. Levin Woothers vs. Job W. Willson and James Richardson. 1860.

230. Louisa B. Breeding vs. John L. Breeding. 1860.

231. William Slay, John Poore, Louis H. Beatty, James H. Temple, William Norris, James H. Scott and Henry Rousset vs. Thomas Straughn admr of William E. Straughn, Elizabeth, Thomas E., Mary, heirs of William E. Straughn. 1860.

232. John Collins and Elizabeth G. his wife and Sarah T. Potter, extrs of Wm. Potter vs. Letitia Andrew, Mary Andrew, Sarah Wright, Zabdial W. Potter, Lucy B. Richardson, Mary R. C. Sipple, Caroline T. Potter, Walter S. Turpin, Sarah Turpin, Ann W. and Wm. Turpin. 1860.

233. John Collins and Elizabeth G. his wife, Sarah T. Potter, extrs of William Potter vs. Tamsey, James Henry, John, William, Elizabeth Ann, Wesley, Mary Ellen, Thomas G. P., Sarah Catharine Towers, and Purnell Todd admr of Henry C. Towers and Zabdial W. Potter and remaining as above. [In his will William Potter mentioned daus: Elizabeth Green Potter, Sarah T. Potter, Maria C. Turpin wife of Dr. Walter S. Turpin, Caroline T. Potter, Mary R. Sipple and son Zabdial W. Potter, and grandchildren, children of decd dau, Susannah: Sally Turpin, Ann W. Turpin.] 1860.

234. Philip Derochbrune [of Minnesota Territories] and Ann C. Newnam [of Caroline Co] vs. William D. and Ann E. Clarke; Laurania Bagan wife of William; Elmira D., Ann Catharine, Julia Newman, and Joshua D., Sally and Julia A. Clarke. [William D. Clarke and Joshua D. Clarke of Illinois. Ann Elizabeth Clarke, Sally Clarke, July A. Clarke of Mississippi. Laurania D.

Bagan wife of William Bagan, formerly Laurania D. Clarke, of Louisiana.
Elmira D. Newman, Ann Catharine Newman and Juliana Newman, of Caroline Co.]
1860.

235. Whiteley Johnson, Isaac Mason, James T. Clark, William A. Barton and
William E. Mason, admr of Andrew Mason vs. (no name). 1860.

236. John T. Sangston vs. Israel Parriss admr of John Parriss, Mary Ann
Parriss, widow, Mary E., Sarah A., George M., Richard A. and Martha J.
Parriss. [John T. Sangston, creditor of John Parriss who d intestate,
leaving Mary Ann Parris widow, Mary E., Sarah A., George M., Richard A. and
Martha J., his children, all under age of 21.] 1860.

237. Arthur J. Willis vs. William H. Reese and Julia Ann his wife. 1860.

238. Susan Clarke vs. Caleb Clarke. 1860.

239. George Bell and Samuel A. Smith and Anna Maria his wife vs. John
Thawley. 1860.

240. George W. Howard and Walter B. Brooke, Elenora Cole and Richard J. Cole
admrs of Abraham G. Cole [decd, of Balt City] vs. William H. Jones. 1860.

241. Nancy Parris vs. Henry Parris. 1860.

242. John Wright and Mary Ann his wife vs. Sarah Stafford. 1860.

243. Arthur J. Willis vs William W. Richardson. 1860.

244. William A. Ford, Clinton Cook and Martha his wife [Marietta Cook his
wife formerly Marietta Ford of Q.A. Co.] vs. Caroline Ford. [of Balt City]
[All above persons possess as tenants in common a farm in lower part of
Caroline Co, adjoining lands of James B. Rumbold.] 1860.

245. Ezra M. Hitch and Mary E. his wife, formerly Wheeler vs. Lydia Ann,
Thomas E., Caleb, Rebecca E. Wheeler. [That Thomas Wheeler late of Caroline
Co d 1845 intestate, leaving Mary E. Wheeler, Lydia Ann Wheeler, Thomas E.
Wheeler, Caleb Wheeler and Rebecca E. Wheeler, his only children. All except
Mary E. are under age of 21.] 1860.

246. Margaret B. Porter widow vs. James W. Thawley and Mary E., his wife,
Margaret B., Francis A., George C., Theophilus W., Richard C. and Arlington
Porter. [Margaret B. Porter is the widow of Francis E. Porter who d May
1858.]

247. Robert E. Hardcastle, Colin T. Hall and wife Mary, James S. Baynard,
Rachel Wright, Walter D. Hardcastle and wife Elizabeth, Henrietta Baynard,
George Baynard, Thomas Baynard, Elijah Harrison, Timothy C. Raymond and
Henrietta his wife, Joseph E. Palmer and Margaret M. his wife, Richard S.
Ralph and Henrietta his wife, Charles Harper and Martha L. his wife vs.
Franklin and Catharine Segar. [Rebecca Wainwright wife of Thomas Wainwright
and formerly Rebecca Brodey, died leaving a son and Thomas her husband. The
son died, then the father died in 1852. Catharine Baynard has since died
intestate unmarried. The estate was distributed as follows: Margaret M.

CHANCERY DOCKET of CAROLINE COUNTY [with annotations]

Palmer 1/12, Henrietta Rolph 1/12, Martha L. Harper 1/12, Robert E.
Hardcastle 1/12 - being children of Sarah Hardcastle. Henrietta Raymond 1/9,
Eliza Harrison 1/9, Benjamin F. Seegar 1/18 and Catharine Seegar 1/18 - being
children of Mary Hardcastle. James S. Baynard 1/24, Thomas H. Baynard 1/24,
George W. Baynard 1/24, Mary Hall 1/24, Rebecca Wright 1/24, Henrietta
Baynard 1/24, Elizabeth Hardcastle 1/24, Catharine Baynard 1/24. B. Franklin
Segar and Catharine Segar, both under age of 21, are the children of Benjamin
Segar of Q.A. Co. George Baynard, Thomas Baynard, Elijah Harrison, Henrietta
Raymond, Margaret M. Palmer and Henrietta Ralph are under age of 21.] 1860.

248. Norris and Lewis Willson vs. Lemuel Causey and James G. Redden. 1860.

249. William W. Reed, Elizabeth W. Cannon, Margaret Robinson, William
Robinson, Mary E. Reed, John Reed, Amelia Reed and William Reed by next
friend, William W. Reed vs. Jesse W. Reed. 1860.

250. John Reese vs. Thomas W. Reese. 1854.

251. Hall Bonwell vs. Caroline and Laura J. Barton. [Hall Bonwell of
Caroline County who is seized of one undivided moiety of a tract called Stock
Landing, 90 acres. The other undivided moiety held by Caroline Barton during
her widowhood with remainder to Laura J. Barton who is under 21 years of
age.] 1856.

252. Charles Culbreth vs. Spencer Hitch Sr., Spencer Hitch Jr., Henry
Straughn, H. H. Stone, officers of Farmers & Merchants Bank of Greensborough. 1858.

253. Martin W. Meloney vs. Jonathan Cahall and Mary Jane his wife, George
Cally and wife Sarah Ann; William W. Meloney; Henry Cannon and Martha Willson
wife of James E. Willson; James E. Meloney; Ada C. Meloney; Elisha Y.
Meloney; Robert F. Meloney and Elizabeth E. Meloney. 1858.

254. George Fisher vs. Alexander J. Taylor extr of Parran Taylor. 1859.

255. Edward Hardcastle vs. Levin Wright. [Edward Hardcastle sold to Levin
Wright on 3 Jan 1855 a tract adjoining lands of late Thomas Wheeler and
others, 120 acres.] 1859.

256. James H. Smith [of Kent Co, Del] vs. Anna M., Maria L. and Alford
Raughley. [William Raughly of Caroline County died 1858 intestate leaving
Ann Maria, Maria L. and Alferd his only children.] 1859.

257. Skinner and Owen Boon vs. Peter Boon. 1854.

258. Benjamin Taylor use of John R. Fountain vs. William T. Ringgold.

259. Jacob Towers vs. Andrew Towers; Mary Nichols; Senah Nichols; John R.
Towers; Catherine Towers; Eliza A. Lane and Hugh Lane. 1860.

260. Richard J. Lockwood vs. Charles B. Jones and wife Araminta.

261. Mary C. Willson vs. Thomas C. Willson. 1860.

262. William D. Voshell and wife Harriet A. and Clementine Voshell vs.
George C. Moore. 1860.

263. William R. Hughlett [of TA. Co] guardian of William Hughlett assignee
of extr of William Hughlett, decd vs. Warner R. Busteed, admr D.B.N. of
Purnell Jump of P., Sarah Greenly, James McClements and Sarah H. his wife,
Philip Warner, Sherwood and George C. Sherwood. [Purnell Jump of P., late of
Caroline Co died 1848 having first on 7 Apirl 1848 made his will on which he
devised to Sarah Greenlee of Caroline Co a farm in Caroline Co and to
children of Solomon Sherwood after the death of Sarah Greenlee. Children of
Solomon Sherwood: Sarah Hellen Sherwood who m James McClements of Kent Co,
Md.; Philip Warner Sherwood; George C. Sherwood of Caroline Co. The
executor, Solomon Sherwood died 28 Nov 1848 whereas Warner R. Busteed was
appointed administrator.]

264. Henry C. Pratt, Mary Pratt and John Charles Pratt vs. Thomas Pratt.

265. John W. Chilcutt and wife Catharine formerly Catharine Harmon and John
W. Harmon vs. Sarah Ann, James S., Isabella, Mary E. Harmon. [James Harmon
died 1854, seized of a tract in lower district of Caroline Co, 246 acres,
leaving widow Ann Harmon and children: Catharine Chilcutt, John W. Harmon,
Sarah Anne Harmon, James L. Harmon, Issebella Harmon, Elenora Harmon and Mary
E. Harmon.

266. Edgar Plummer and George W. Thawley admrs of John Thawley vs. Thomas
W. Pritchett and wife Martha. John Thawley died intestate after 21 July
1852.

267. Stephen Redden [of Kent Co, Del.) vs. James Redden, Henry Carey, Ginsey
Hall, Mary Carey, Hetty Nicholson, William Redden, Nehemiah Redden, Sally
Redden, Mary Redden, Benton Prettyman, Beniah Jones, Jese Jones, George
Jones, Elizabeth Jones, Charles Jones, James Wheeler, Rhoda Ann Wheeler,
William Spicer, John Spicer, James Spicer, Elizabeth Hazzard, Purnell
Petterjohn, Mary Petterjohn, James Petterjohn, --- Walker, Nancy Donovan,
Edward V. Davis, Hiram Davis, Mary Ann Davis, Harrison Davis, Nancy Davis,
Sarah Davis, John Davis, Hellen Caroline Lindall, Mary Davis, John D. Ingram
and Trustine Coulter. [Nehemiah Redden of Sussex Co, Del., died intestate
around Dec 1854 seized of a tract, Gabrels Landing in Caroline Co. He never
married, no issue. Surviving him are 3 half-brothers, 3 half- sisters, and
issue of one half-brother and 4 half-sisters, that is to say: James Redden,
Stephen Redden, Henry Carey, Ginsey Carey who m Robert Hall, Mary Carey,
Hetty Carey who m Thomas Nicholson, William Redden who died in the lifetime
of the intestate leaving children: William Redden, Nehemiah Redden, Sally
Redden and Mary Redden, Amelia Redden who m Robert Prettyman and afterwards
Thomas Jones and died in the lifetime of the intestate leaving to survive her
as her children, Burton Prettyman, William Prettyman, Beniah Jones and Jesse
Jones, Betty Redden who m William Spicer and died in lifetime of intestate
leaving to survive her children, Nancy Spicer who m Brinkley Davis and died
in lifetime of intestate leaving to survive her children, John Davis and Mary
Davis; and Nancy Carey who m John Coulter and died in lifetime of intestate
leaving to survive her as her children, Tristine Coulter, all of which said
parties reside out of the state of Maryland.]

268. William Newlee vs. Simeon West, Hannah West, Elizabeth Newlee, Charles
Gibson, Martha Gibson, William N. Scott, Sarah Scott, Eliza Newlee, Charles
Edward Newlee, William Franklin Newlee and Henry Newlee. [Keziah Newlee died
intestate leaving a farm which was formerly the property of James Newlee and
which was purchased by Keziah Newlee from commissioners appointed to value
and divide real estate of James Newlee, 230 acres; and a farm, 240 acres,
which descended to her from her father, Edward Swift, being his home farm.
Keziah Newlee died leaving son William Newlee and dau Hannah who m Simeon
West, dau Elizabeth Newlee, dau Martha who m Charles Gibson, dau Sarah who m
William N. Scott, Eliza Newlee, William Franklin Newlee, Charles Edward
Newlee and Henry Newlee, her grandchildren, infant children of her deceased
son Warner Newlee.]

269. Elizabeth, William, John, Caleb Wright and Lilly Adams and Elisha
Wright vs. William H., Andrew S. S., Horatio W., Jesse T., Virginia C.
Wright, Thomas Lewis and Sela his wife, Rice Gambrill and Mary Ann his wife,
William E. Todd and John Willson and Sarah Ann his wife, John Lord and Jane
his wife and Caleb James Todd. [Horatio Wright of Caroline Co died Jan 1858
leaving widow, Sallie, no children, and brothers and sisters, William H.
Wright, Andrew S. L. Wright, Horatio H. Wright, Jesse T. Wright and Virginia
C. Wright, children of Peter Wright, a deceased brother of Horatio Wright,
Sela Lewis wife of Thomas Lewis, Mary Ann Gambrill wife of Rice Gambrill,
William E. Todd, Sarah Ann Willson wife of John Willson, John Wesley Todd,
Jane Lord wife of John Lord and Caleb James Todd children of Mary Todd
deceased sister of said Horatio. Virginia C. Wright and Caleb J. Todd are
under age of 21 years. Horatio's widow Sallie resides in 2d district of
Caroline Co where her husband died. The following live in 4th district of
Caroline Co: William Wright, Caleb Wright, Elisha Wright, Betey Wright and
Lilly Adams wife of Thomas Adams deceased. John Wright lives in the middle
district.]

270. Henry Roussett vs. Charles and Henry Stubbs, John Russell, Ann
Williams, Priscilla McCalley and Andrew Stubbs. [John Stubbs of Caroline Co
died Dec 1850 intestate leaving 2 sons: Henry and Charles; 2 daus: Priscilla
McCally and Ann Williams; and a grandson, John Russell infant son of Mahalla
Stubbs, deceased.

271. Joseph W. Brown [of TA. Co] vs. John Dean and Robert Thomas. [Joseph
W. Brown by his marriage with Rachael F. Reese, dau of Garretson Reese, late
of Caroline Co, deceased, he and Rachael are seized of a tract in lower
district of Caroline Co, Alcock's Chance, 11 acres. Garretson Reese died
1849.]

272. James Anderson vs. John Anderson.

273. John T. Sangston vs. James C., Shadrack, William, Roderick, Mary and
Eliza Harper.

274. Wm. B. Massey vs. Mary Dukes, Azriel S. Reyner, John Boon Reyner and
Sallie P. Reyner.

275. Charles Dean vs. Lilly Ann, Wm., Charles, Sarah E. Harriet E. and Ann
E. P. Murphy.

276. Ennalls Hubbard, guardian vs. John, James and Martena Carroll.

277. Charles E. Tarr, guardian vs. William, Sarah and Mary Sullivan (free negroes)

278. Isaiah C. Blades vs. Samuel Hubbard. Oct 1861.

279. John F. Moffett, Richard Mocklen, Jacob Hoff, under name of Moffett, Mocklen & Hoff vs. James K. Saulsbury. Oct 1861.

280. Henry R. Pratt, Mary Pratt and John Charles Pratt vs. Thomas Pratt. March 1862. [Henry R. Pratt and Mary his wife of the city of Baltimore and John Charles Pratt of California. Ann Pratt of QA Co died 1833 seized of real estate in Q.A. Co and Caroline Co. In her will she devised real estate to her grandchildren: Charles Pratt and Thomas W. Pratt. Exhibit of will of Ann Pratt mentions grandson Henry J. F. Pratt and his sisters Charlotte Ann Wright, Alizira Wright and Ellen F. Pratt; grandson Thomas Pratt and Edwin E. Pratt (relationship?) who is under 21 years of age, and great grandson Lemuel Wright and wife, Fanny and her brother. Also mentioned slaves: Tom; Phil; Maria; Margaret; Charlotte; Cassander (boy), Mary and child; Fanny and child; Daniel; Hesse (woman); Henry; Maria; Lambert; Thadeas; Lott; Mingo; Theodore; and Charles.]

281. John R. F. Saulsbury vs. Bennett Wherrett, infant. March 1862.

282. John W. Chilcutt and Catharine his wife, formerly Catharine Harmon, and John W. Harmon vs. Sarah Ann, James L., Josebella and Mary E. Harmon. March 1862.

283. Willis Corkran vs. Eugene M. Corkran. March 1862.

284. James Payne, guardian of John H. Reese vs. John H. Reese, infant. 1862

285. Albert W. Davis vs. Paul Conoway. 1862.

286. John W. Stevens vs. Daniel G., Francis G., Mary J., William H., James, Martha J. and William J. Stevens; and James H., John L., Andrew T., Mary A. and Francis E. Sullivan. [William Stevens of Caroline Co died 1844 leaving fol children: David G. Stevens, Francis G. Stevens, Mary Jane Stevens and Nancy J. wife of Andrew Towers; and his grandchildren: William H. Stevens son of James C. Stevens a deceased son of William Stevens; James and Martha Stevens children of Samuel T. Stevens a deceased son of William Stevens; William J. Stevens son of Solomon B. Stevens a deceased son of William Stevens; and James H. Stevens; John S. Sullivan, Mary H. Sullivan, Andrew S. Sullivan, Francis E. Sullivan, children of Sally Sullivan, decd, dau of William Stevens and wife of Andrew Sullivan. 1862.

287. Peter and Tilghman Andrew vs. Celia, Henrietta, Sarah Ann and Isaac Andrew. 1862.

288. William G. Vanstavern and Frances A. his wife vs. Thomas F. Garey, trustee of Ennalls Hubbard and Ellen T. his wife. 1862.

289. Charles and Hellen V. Nutter vs. Alexander Gardner. [Alleged that Alexander Gardner of Caroline Co, father of Helen V. Nutter is of unsound mind.] 1862.

290. James W. Thawly and Mary E., his wife, vs. Margaret B., Francis A., George C., Theopholus W., Richard C. and Arlington Porter. 1862.

291. Charles H. Todd vs. William and Clement Todd; Elizabeth and Thomas Dynes; Alexander Todd; Laura Turner; William F., Thomas H. Ann W. and Eliza W. Todd. 1862.

292. Robert, David, George W. and Shadrach J. Raughley; Daniel H. Robinson and Margaret E., his wife vs. Ann Raughley, widow; Ann Maria, Mary Laura, Alfred, James F. and Ary Ann Raughley. 1862.

293. Thomas F. Garey vs. William Morgan and Clement Sullivan. 1862.

294. Mary E. Corkran and Thomas F., her husband vs George W. and Frances A. Camper. 1862.

295. Eliza Jane Williams next friend to Williamina F., Luther and Ella Moore Williams, infants vs. Joshua Seward and Mary W. his wife. 1862.

296. William Chesnutt and S. P. Townsend under the firm of Wm. Chestnutt & Co., vs. John T. Sangston.

297. Joseph Turner vs. Matthew J. Clarke. 1862.

298 Richard Greenwell vs. Jonathan Evetts & A. Y. Collins. 1862.

299. Peter O. Cherbonnier extr of John Evetts vs. Ennalls Hubbard, Tilghman Andrew, Samuel Thomas and Bethany his wife, James and Mary Mobray, William Lain and Priscilla his wife. 1863.

300. James H. Holmes vs. George and Frances A. Camper. 1863.

301. William A. R. Griffith and Ann M., his wife, vs. Mary R. Griffith, William A. Ford, Thomas Henry Ford, Mariah Louisa, Ann Josephine, Lucy Potter, Mary Ringrose and William R. Griffith. 1863.

302. George E. Sangston vs. James Gooding and Mary his wife and Warner R. Busteed. 1863.

303. Joshua McGonigal, guardian, vs. James P. and John Coursey, infants. 1863.

304. A. J. Willis vs. Martin Price and Purnell Todd. 1863.

305. Alexander Knotts vs. John Stafford and Nancy his wife. 1863.

306. Thomas H. Kemp Jr. vs. Francis Willson. 1863.

307. Milton Cooper, William M. Parham and Robert D. Work under the firm of Style & Cooper, Parham & Work, vs. William Genn and Susan his wife and John W. Simpson. 1863.

308. William P. Richardson, Thomas C. Watkins, Francis D. Dungan, George F. R. Waeschee, under the firm of Watkins, Dungan & Waeschee, vs. Thomas, Tilghman, Samuel, William, Abraham N. and Maria Collins and Charles

Saulsbury and Sarah A. his wife; Richard Andrew of Luke; Ennalls Hubbard,
Josiah, James E., John Wesley and Elizabeth Collins of James; George H. and
Ary Ann Collins, minors; Thomas Andrew and Nancy his wife; Elizabeth Collins
of H., minor; Laurania, Niccy, Francis and Sarah Ellen Collins; Charles A.
Griffith admr of John Collins; Thomas and Jesse Collins; Robert Harris and
Mary Edna his wife. 1863.

309. William and Robert Rawley vs Manlove Jester. 1863.

310. Andrew and Jacob Towers vs. Seney Nicols and Mary his wife, John R.,
Catharine, Lucretia and Eliza A. Towers. 1863.

311. Joshua McGonigal for use of Samuel McGonigal vs. James E. Imbert.
1863.

312. James H. and Eliza A. Lane vs. Poulson E. Hubbard & James G. Redden.
1863.

313. Ennalls Hubbard vs. Charles H. Todd and Alexander Knotts, late sheriff
of Caroline Co. 1863.

314. James Stafford vs. Ennalls A., Martha J. and Mary L. Breeding, Emeline
Ferrins and Thomas Ferrins. 1863.

315. Charles H. Todd admr of Thomas Todd vs. Thomas F. Garey and Francis D.
Dungan. 1863.

316. Charles E. Jarrell and James E. Hignutt vs. Ennalls Hubbard and Ellen
T. his wife. 1863.

317. Charles E. Jarrell and James E. Hignutt vs. Ennalls Hubbard. 1863.

318. Jesse W. Reed use of S. H. Smith use of H. C. Comegys use of R. C.
Carter vs. Jeremiah Irving. 1863.

319. Arthur J. Willis vs. James B. Selby and Williamina his wife. 1863.

320. Jacob Charles vs. Josiah, Thomas C. Collins and Henrietta his wife.
1863.

INDEX

69

BECHAMP Thomas 26
Bee Tree Swamp 28
Beetree Corrected 23
Beginning, The 5, 20, 43
BELL --- 14
  Cyrus 32, 45
  Daniel 23, 32, 54
  Fanny 28
  George 5, 61
  Henry 32
  James 5, 6, 21
  John Stevens 14
  Joshua 53
  Joshua C. 54
  Margaret 32
  Nancy 32
  Robert 32, 42
  Samuel 19
  Sarah 32, 45
  Selby 28
  Thomas 5, 9, 19
  William 2, 4, 12, 32
Benjamin's Desire 10
BENNET Tolson 40
BENNETT John 17, 18, 19,
  20, 22
  Thomas 10
Bennett's Tolson 13
Bennetts Purchase 11
BERRY Major 12
  Margaret E. 57
Betsey's Range 14
Betsys Care 10
Bett's Range 14
BETTS Harriet E. 57
  Samuel 57
Betty Carol's branch 11
Beulah Lot 43
BILLETER John 22
  Joseph 20
Billeter's Landing 21
BIRCH Grove 31
BISHOP Mary Amanda 41
  Richard 41
  Robert 14, 54
  William 16
Bite the Biter 31
Black Level Enlarged 32
BLACK Mary 49
  Philip 35
  Robert 35, 49
  Wiliana 35
BLACKWELL Joseph 1, 7

BLADES Alexander 49
  Arnold 11
  Eliza Ann 46, 49
  Garretson 46, 49
  Hixon 47
  Isaiah C. 59, 65
  James 11
  Joseph 12
  Levin 12, 18, 22, 49
  Mary 19
  Nancy 49
  Susan 59
  Thomas 12, 49
  Traphena 47
  William 19
BLAIR Charles 12, 14,
  15, 16, 17
BLAKE Deborah 18
  Frances 38, 45
  John W. 38, 45
  William 18, 38, 45
BLAND Joseph 1, 19
Bloomsberry 11
BLUNT Benjamin 14
  Levi 22
  Lydia 22
BONWELL Hall 62
  Louisa 35
  William 35
Booby Owl Farm 43
BOON Abraham 9
  Ann 35
  Charles Edmond 38
  Charlotte 35
  Elizabeth 27, 35
  Hawkins 9
  Hawkins H. 27
  Isaac 9, 10, 13, 15,
  26
  Jacob 4, 9, 11, 13,
  25
  James 9, 13, 15, 20,
  25, 26
  James M. 36
  John 14, 22, 25, 26,
  27, 28, 35, 36, 52,
  53, 54, 55
  John Francis 38
  Joseph 9, 15, 26, 27,
  28, 33, 36, 60
  Joshua 34, 36, 38
  Juliana 35
  Kitty Driver 35
  Lenora 35
  Mary Elizabeth 35

  Matilda 36
  Moses 9, 26
  Owen 62
  Peter 62
  Rebecca 34, 38
  Skinner 62
  Susan 36
  Thomas 18, 22
  William 9, 10, 13, 25,
  26, 35
Boon's Court 31
Boon's Hazard 28
Boon's Park 9, 25, 36
Boon's Pleasure 27, 31
Boon's Purchase 13
Boon's Venture 13
BOONE Jacob 14
BORDLEY John W. 48
BOURKE Edward 17
  Elizabeth 17
  Mary 17
  Nathan 17
  Sarah 17
  Thomas 17
  Thomas F. 55
BOWDLE Caleb 36
  Joseph 10
  Margaret 36
  Thomas 10
BOWIE Isabella Dallas 51
  Joseph Haskins 51
  Josephine Haskins 51
  Louiza Emaly 51
BOWLEY John W. 44
BOYCE William 59
BOYER Caleb 20
BOZMAN Elizabeth 29
  George 29
  Henrietta 29
  John 18, 29
  Jonathan 18
  Lucretia 29
  Maccabees 29
  Mr. 20
  Philemon 29
BRACCO John 6
BRADLEY Caroline 34
  Charles 15
  John 34
  Nathan 15
  Sarah 34
  Stephen 34
  William 1
Bradley Farm 43
Bradley's Addition 34

INDEX

Mary 48
Price N. 48
Sally Ann 48
Susan 48
DEIN Levin 26
DELEHAY Elizabeth 37
DELEHAY William 37, 56
Denby 16
DENNY Benjamin 22
Denton's Valley 5, 28
DERICKSON James 32
Mary 32
DEROACHBRUNE Almira 56
Ann 56
Ann C. 56
Ellen G. 56
John 23
Peregrine 23
Philip 56
Sarah 23
DEROCHBROUNE Margaret 41
DEROCHBRUNE John 14
Matthew 14
Philip 60
Philip S. 51
DICKINSON Charles 4, 10,
19
Deborah 19
Henry 2, 3, 4, 5, 7, 8,
10, 26
James 19
John 13, 15, 17, 19
Samuel 8, 10, 17
William 1, 2, 3
Dickinson's land 16
Dickinson's Plains 25,
27, 31, 33
DILL Thomas 10
DILLEN Ann 25
James 19
John 25, 30
Mark 30
Mary 30
Vinson 29
DILLING Joshua 19
DILLON Elizabeth 49
James 41, 49, 56
Jane 49, 56
John 41, 49, 56
Mary 49, 56
Nancy 49, 56
Sarah 49
Susan 41, 49, 56
William 30, 41, 49, 56
DINES Joshua 7

DINKLE William 13
Discovery, The 17, 31
DIXON James 16
Obediah 11
Robert 5, 11
Dockeray's Meadows 30
Doctor's Fancy 28
DONOVAN Nancy 63
Double Purchase 32
DOUGLASS Ann E. 43
James E. 42, 43
James H. 43
Joseph 14, 15, 43
Samuel E. 43
Stephen E. 43
Thomas H. 27, 43
DOWNES Aaron 3, 5, 6,
9, 13, 17, 20, 21
Ann 17, 45
Ann W. 55
Elizabeth 6, 15
Ellen T. 43
Emeline 38
Hawkins 3, 20, 21
Henrietta 17
Henry 1, 2, 4, 5, 6,
7, 8, 11, 12, 13, 14,
16, 17, 20, 22, 23,
24
James 17
James M. 55
John 38, 43
John A. 43
Margaret 6
Nathan 5, 6, 17
Philemon 3, 4, 5, 6,
8, 11, 13, 15, 17
William 41, 45
William H. 41
DRAPER Ann 50
Elisha 50
Ephriam 28
John 47
Judal 5
Judril 28
Lewis 28, 45, 47
Margaret 47
Mary 47
R. J. 59
Rebecca 47
Samuel 47
DRIVER Alford 50
Christopher 6, 11,
18, 19, 35
Eliza Ann 50

Elizabeth 45
Henry 28, 45, 50, 54
Hester Ann 50
James 50, 54
John 50
John R. 54
Joshua 28, 45, 50
Lucian 50
Lukean 54
Margaret 45
Mary 35, 50
Matthew 5, 7, 8, 16,
19, 28, 49, 50, 54
Mrs. 18
Peregrine R. 35
Theodore 54
Theodore Denny 50
Drum Field 12
Dry Savannah 14
Dublin 11, 20
DUDLEY George 6
Dudley's Chance 1
Dudley's Desire 16
DUKE John 41
Sally Ann 41
Duke's Enterprise 40
Dukedom 43
DUKES Ann 26, 53
Ann M. 55
Anna 51
Daniel 51
Elizabeth 39
Isaac 56
Isaac R. 39
James 39, 50, 53, 55
James Kent 39
John Boon 39
Levi 24, 26, 27, 29,
46, 56
Levi T. 39
Levin 58
Mary 56, 64
Rebecca Ellen 39
Sarah 21
Susan 58
Thomas 7
William 26, 28
DULANEY William 14
Duncaster 24, 26
DUNGAN Francis D. 66, 67
DUNLAP Silas 54
DUNNING Samuel 59
DWIGANS Ann 20
James 21
John 8

76

77

INDEX

78

INDEX

Rachel 33
Susan 33
William 33
Joans Thickett 6
John Steven's Mill 12
John's Chance 17
JOHNSON Cornelius 7
  Dr. S. T. 19
  Henry 28
  James 26, 46
  John 24
  Levin 27
  Mary 24
  Tilghman 28, 56
  Whiteley 61
Johnson's Delight 28
Johnson's Entrance 28
Jone's Forest 8
Jone's Forrest 15
Jones Addition to Good
  Hope 40
JONES Allanora 38
  Anna Maria 57
  Araminta 62
  Beniah 63
  Benjamin F. 57
  Bennett 41
  Charles 19, 24, 63
  Charles B. 57, 62
  Curtis M. 54
  Elizabeth 63
  Forest 2
  George 63
  Henrietta 57
  James D. 57
  James M. 42
  Jesse 63
  John 41
  Joseph B. 57
  Maria 50, 53
  Mariah 52
  Mary 41
  Mary E. 42
  Mary Louisa 41
  Richard 38, 47
  Richard J. 47
  Robert 6, 20
  Sacht 12
  Sally B. 57
  Sarah Elizabeth 54
  Susan 58
  Thomas 42, 58, 63
  William 10, 13, 17, 38,
  41, 50, 52, 53, 54, 55,
  57

William H. 61
William L. 41
William Wallace 57
Jones Forest 2
JORDAN Robert 5
Joseph's Lott 1
JOSHUA D. 60
JUMP Abraham 19, 52, 54
  Alemby 4, 22, 25, 28,
  29
  Andrew 29
  Ann 54
  Benjamin 4, 5, 16
  Elijah 4, 54
  Helena 35
  Henrietta 35
  Henry 31
  Isaac 35
  John 5, 22, 35, 54,
  56
  Levin 7
  Mahala 35
  Martha 35
  Mary 35, 51
  Nathan 9
  P. 56, 63
  Peter 4, 5, 7, 9, 10,
  54
  Purnell (Purnall) 4,
  63
  Sarah 19
  Sarah Jane 55
  Solomon 4
  Susanna 5
  Thomas 2, 4, 5, 7, 9,
  16
  Vaughn 5
  William 2, 4, 5, 29,
  52
  Zachariah 54
Jump's Chance 5, 19
Jump's Choice 23
Jump's Lane 16
Jump's Lot 29, 31

KEENE Catharine E. 41,
  58
  James 29, 49
  John 23, 24
  Marcellus 55
  Margaret 48
  Mary S. 55
  Richard 23, 25
  Robert 48
  Robert T. 35

Sally Ann 41
Thomas Billingsley 1
William A. 46
William B. 23
KEETS William 4
KEIRN Nathan 48
KELLEY Dennis 29
  James 56
  Sally 56
KELLY Ann 32, 41
  Dennis 44, 46
  Hannah 44, 46
  Hicks 44, 46
  James 41
  Martin 44, 46
  Paulson 32
  Rachel 31, 44
  Sarah 41
  Sylvester 44, 46
  William 12, 31, 32, 44
KEMP Henry 3
  Thomas H. 66
KENNARD Richard 18
KENT Solomon 21
KENTON Elizabeth 17
  Henry 17, 23, 38
  Howel 17
  James 12, 17
  Lydia 17
  Solomon 3, 11, 12, 13,
  17, 20
  Thomas 12
  William 38
Kill Maiden 23, 40
Kill Maiden's Addition 40
Kilray 5
Kilray's Addition 5
KINDERDINE Cooper 23
KING Henry G. 53, 55
  John 12
  Nanette 53
  Nanette 55
KINNAMON Mary Ellen 57
  Sorden 57
KINNEMON Samuel 20
KINNEMONT Joseph 17
  Margaret 17
KIRBY Robert 6
  Stephen 9
KIRKHAM James 3
Kirkham's Discovery 30,
  34, 56
Kirkham's Garden 2
Kirkham's Lott 2, 11

82

KIRKMAN Elizabeth 22
  William 22
KIRWIN James 47
  Nathan 47
  Richard 47
Kitturage Doctor 15
KNOTTS Absalom 4
  Alexander 59, 60
  Alexander 66
  Alexander 67
  Captain
  James 15
  Nathaniel 1, 6, 7, 9,
  13
Knotts Range 7
LADMORE --- 2
LAIN Charles 58
  Priscilla 66
  William 66
Lain's Folly 13
Laine's Addition 34
LAMBDIN Ann Maria 48
  George 48
  Henry 48
Lambert 2, 11, 65
Lambert's Addition 11
LAMDON Ann Maria 48
  George 48
  Henry 48
Lamp High 40
LANCE Sarah C. 59
LANE --- 6
  Charles 59
  Eliza A. 62, 67
  Hugh 62
  James H. 67
  John 2, 5, 6, 9, 10,
  11, 13
  John F. 59
  Rachel E. 59
  Richard 19
  Richard E. 59
  Sarah C. 59
  Timothy 11
  Walter 6, 13
Lane's Folly 6, 13
Lane's Ridge 28
Lane's Venture 40
LANGSTRETH and BAILEY 60
Large Range 14
Last Vacancy 28
LATCHUM Eliza Ann 29
  Kendall 29
  Margaret 29
  Maria 29

  Nodera 29
  Sarah 29
  Winlock 29
LAWS George 55
LAYNE James 4
  John 5
  Walter 5
Laynes Addtn 4
LAYTON John 18
Lazy Hill 7
LEARY Charles 51
  John 51
  Philemon 51
  Sarah 51
  Wharton 51
LEATH John 24
LECOMPT James 18
  Thomas 18
LECOMPTE Charles 8, 17,
  19
  Edward E. 44
  Elizabeth 28
  James 7, 8, 19, 28
  John 1, 7
  Mary Ann Eliza 47
  Priscilla 28
  Sally Caroline 47
  Samuel 28
  Sarah 28
  Thomas 19, 28
Lecompte's Lot 32
Lecompte's Regulation
  28
LEGG Nancy 28
  Richard 28
LEMARE Gallant 25
LEVENUS Rice 13, 17
LEVERING Enoch 46
  Jesse 46
  Nathan 46
LEVERTON Hannah C. 53
  Jacob 53
  John 16
  Thomas 4, 11, 16
Levin's Folly Enlarged
  27
LEWIS Abraham 18
  Sela 64
  Thomas 15, 18, 64
LIDEN Ann Adams 36
  Edward W. 36, 41
  Elizabeth E. 41
  Elizabeth Emily 36
  Sarah A. 41
  Sarah R. 41

  Shadrack 36
  William E. 41
  William M. A. 36
LIGHTON Shadrack 21
LINDALL Hellen Caroline
  63
LISTER John 15
LLOYD Colonel 16
  Edward 8
Lloyd's Forest 20
Lloyd's Kindness 21
Lloyd's Regulation 6, 18,
  22, 28, 32, 34, 35, 38,
  41
Lloyds Grove 29
LOCKE Thomas M. 46
LOCKWOOD Richard J. 62
Logan's (Loggins) Horns
  40, 60
LONG Eliza 31
  Samuel 31
Long Marsh Ridge 41
Long Marsh Ridge Enlarged
  33
LONGFELLOW Amos 33
  John 15, 33
LONGSTREET Samuel 47
LOOCKERMAN Jacob 5, 8, 9,
  13, 19
  John 13
  Rebecca 58
  Richard 2, 3, 5, 6, 7,
  8, 9, 13, 58
  Stanley 19
  Thomas 15, 17, 58, 59
  Thomas Wynn 13, 20
  William 58
Loockerman's Beginning 29
Loockerman's Purchase 24
LORD Alexander 42
  Alexander W. 42
  Jane 64
  John 64
  Martha J. 42
Lot, The 31
LOTT 65
LOVE William 9
LOVEDAY Thomas 12
LOWE Elizabeth 5
LUCAS Ann 41, 49
  Maria 29
  Michael 11
  Samuel 29
  Stephen 26
  William 41, 49

84

Caleb 32
Charity 32
Charles 39
James 39
Jane 39
Joshua 39
Levin 18, 32
Mark 42, 52
Mary 44
Nathan 32
Sarah 39
Solomon 39
Summers 32
Twiford 39
William 32, 39
NOEL Thomas 2, 11, 16
NORRIS Martin 23
William 23, 25, 60
NORVILL Robert 33
Nowell's land 15
NUTTER Charles 1, 65
David 1
Hellen V. 65
John 1
Mary 1
William 1
NUTTERWELL Daniel 8

Oak Ridge 25
Old Boone's, The 2
Old Town(e) 1, 14
OLDFIELD Elijah G. 53
John 53
Merriam A. B. 53
William 53
ORELL William 28
ORRELL Daniel 36, 59
Durdin 12
Francis 13
Henry 41
Mary 32
Rebecca 36, 59
Robert 16, 22, 23, 25,
27, 28, 33, 41
Robert J. 41
William 25, 26, 27, 32
Orrell's Chance 41
Ottowottocoquin 1
Out Range 16, 21, 27, 31,
32, 41, 42
OVERSTOCKS Elizabeth 21
OWEN Edmond 51
Margaret 51
OWENS William 1

OXENHAM Elizabeth 20
Hester Ann 49
Mary 49
Mordecai 49
Richard 17
William 21, 49
William Henry 49

PAINE Amelia 36
Catherine 36
George 36
Henrietta 36
James 36
William 36
Painter's Mistake 29
Painter's Range 19, 23,
42
PALMER Joseph E. 61
Margaret M. 61, 62
PARHAM & WORK 66
PARHAM William M. 66
PARK James 6
Peters 6
Parke's Freshes 17
PARKER William 2, 3
Parker's Freshes 20
PARRIS Henry 61
Joseph 44
Mahala 44
Mary Ann 61
Nancy 61
PARRISS George M. 61
Israel 61
John 61
Martha J. 61
Mary Ann 61
Mary E. 61
Richard A. 61
Sarah A. 61
PARROTT William 28
Parrott's Lookout 33
Partnership 4, 24, 25,
31, 34
Partnership Hazzard 12
Partnership in Fishing
Pleasant Red Oak Pond
21
PATTERSON Joseph W. 48
PATTISON Joseph W. 50
PATTON Barrett 58
Matthew 42
PAYNE James 65
PEARCE James 22, 23, 25
PEARSON Ann 49
Caroline 35

John 16
Joseph 38
Maria 41
Peter 35
Sarah 41
Sarah Ann 38
Sarah C. 41
Thomas 6, 16, 29, 49
William T. 41
Pearson's Chance 16
PENDLETON Edmond 31
Isaac Purnell 31, 52
Serena 31
Serena C. 52
Serena Catharine 31
PENINGTON Thomas 14
PENNINGTON Thomas 5, 6,
7, 15, 17
PERRY Richard 10
Thomas 4, 10, 17
William 10, 11, 17
Perry's Desire 30
Perry's Flintshire 30
Perry's Grove 29
Perrys Purchase Part 10
PERT John 8
Peter's Exceptible Lot 31
Peter's Purchase 26
PETERS Anderton 47
Chaney 47
Charles 56
Keturah 39
Maria 47
Nancy 47
Peters Park 6
PETTERJOHN James 63
Mary 63
Purnell 63
PHIL 65
PICKIRIN John 12
PIERSON Betsey 16
Piney Neck 33
Piney Neck Regulated 32,
34
Piney Point 12, 18, 42
PINKINE Michael 56
PIPPIN Benjamin 23
Derias 28
Henrietta 52
James 45, 52
John 28
Joseph 28, 52
Solomon 28
Thomas 42
Tristram 45

INDEX

89

INDEX

Morgan 33
Nancy 32
Neglect 29
Richard 25
Robert 16, 21
Sally Thomas 33
Samuel 6
widow 16
Wilhimenia T. 42
William 32
Williamina F. 66
WILLIAMSON Clousberry 22
Elijah 14
Willingsborough 15
Willinle 31
WILLIS A. J. 66
Arthur J. 42, 61, 67
Arthur John 56
Elizabeth 4
Henry 23
Henry F. 42
Isaac 17, 19, 20
Jarvis 20
John 4, 10, 13, 17, 19, 20
John G. 55
Jonathan 20
Joshua 2, 3, 4, 7, 11, 12, 14, 16, 17, 18
Levin 23
Mary 42
Mary E. 42
Peter J. 42
Philip 17
Richard S. 42
Sarah 52
Short A. 42, 53
Thomas 46
Thomas Foster 52
WILLOUGHBY Absalum 28
Anthony 16
Edward 12, 16
R. J. 59
Richard 16, 22
William 22
WILLSON Balseray 56
Christopher 25
Daniel 56
Elenah 56
Elijah 53
Elisha 53
Elkany 56
Ellender 39
Francis 66
Jacob C. 53

James 21, 53
James E. 62
Job 56
Job W. 55, 56, 60
John 15, 21, 64
Jonathan 56
Lewis 62
Martha 62
Martha E. 53
Mary 24
Mary C. 62
Norris 62
Rachael 56
Richard A. 24
Robert E. 57
Sarah Ann 64
Thomas 24
Thomas Bennett 3
Thomas C. 57, 62
William 1, 57
WILMER Pere 54, 56
Peregrine 53
WILSON Allen 28
Ann 18, 30, 38
Balseray 50
Daniel 50
Eliza 38
Elkany 50
Hester 38
James 17, 18
Job 50
John 18, 38, 47
Jonathan 16, 50
Lewis 50
Margaret 18
Mary 50
Peter 30
Rachel 50
Rachel J. 38
Rebecca 38
Rebecca Ann 38
Robert 18, 38
Sarah 18, 57
Solomon 17
Sterling 47
Thomas 3
Thomas M. 38
William 18, 21, 38, 46
Wiltshire 31
Winchester's Folly 15
Winchester's Folly Resurveyed 15
WING Thomas 18, 23
WINSLOW John 10

WM. CHESTNUTT & Co. 66
WOOD Ann 52
Jasper 19
Joseph 52
WOOLFORD David 3, 7, 8, 9, 10, 12, 16, 21
Joanna 21
Philip 21, 26, 27
WOOLMAN Mary 37
Woolverton 11
Wooters Choice Resurveyed 30
WOOTERS Jacob 4
Jonathan 6
Lemuel 14
Levin 38, 56
Mary Ellen 38
Matthew 38
Nancy 16
Sarah 38
Sarah Jane 38
WOOTHERS John 16
Levin 60
WOOTTERS Levin 35
Thomas 5
WORK Robert D. 66
World's End 18
WRIGHT A. 44
Alizira 65
Amelia 58
Andrew S. L. 64
Andrew S. S. 64
Ann 31, 45
Ann Elizabeth 38
Aramintha 42
Caleb 38, 64
Celia 42, 45
Charles 42, 44
Charlotte Ann 65
Daniel 14, 31, 44, 45, 47
Delia 36
Edward 45, 46
Elisha 34, 64
Elizabeth 41, 56, 64
Fanny 65
Harris 45
Hatfield 27, 47
Horatio 64
Horatio H. 64
Horatio W. 64
Isaac 34, 58
Isaac K. 41
Jacob 27, 34, 45, 46
James 14, 45, 46

95

www.ingramcontent.com/pod-product-compliance
Lightning Source LLC
LaVergne TN
LVHW021539080426
835509LV00019B/2738